DYNAMICS OF THE SELF

DYNAMICS
OF
THE SELF

Gerhard Adler

Coventure Ltd

Published by Coventure Ltd, London

Copyright © 1979 by Gerhard Adler

ISBN 0 904576 7681 7

Typeset by Red Lion Setters, Holborn, London
Printed and bound in Great Britain by
The Anchor Press Ltd

*To my wife, children and grandchildren who have been
the blessings of my life*

Contents

Preface   i

Basic Concepts of Analytical Psychology   1

The Dynamics of the Self   15

The Logos of the
Unconscious   33

Ego Integration and
Patterns
of the Coniunctio   52

On the Question of
Meaning
in Psychotherapy   62

Personal Encounters
with Jung
and his work   88

Depth Psychology and the
Principle of Complementarity   103

Remembering and
Forgetting   119

Preface

A volume of papers stretching over almost thirty years requires some explanation of its purpose and general theme. It lies in the fact that a common subject underlies all of them: the creative powers of the psyche and of the workings of the self, and of the process of individuation. These points run like a red thread through the various chapters of the book.

The essays have not been arranged in their time sequence but rather according to their subject matter, in what I hope will appear as a logical — or psycho-logical — sequence.

Thus the first paper on "Basic Concepts of Analytical Psychology" appears as a kind of introductory essay, giving the basis for the following chapters. It tries to communicate to an interested public, not necessarily too well informed about details of the main tenets of Analytical Psychology, the foundation for the following essays. It was written for the Guild of Pastoral Psychology, London, and published as *Guild Lecture No.174* in April 1974.

The three following papers present practical examples of the application of these basic concepts. There is first of all the chapter which has given the book its thematic title: "The Dynamics of the Self". It illustrates the rôle of the self in the case of a child and of an adult, comparing the two. It was read originally in 1950 to the Medical Section of the British Psychological Society (and published in the *British Journal of Medical Psychology*, vol.XXIV, pt.2, 1951).

The second paper in this series, entitled "The Logos of the Unconscious", shows the "intellectual activity of the unconscious", manifesting itself in an intelligent and purposive process directed by the self. This paper was originally published in 1955 as a contribution to the *Festschrift* on the occasion of Jung's 80th birthday (in *Studien zur Analytischen Psychologie C.G. Jungs*, Zürich, 1955). A related subject is illustrated by the case of a middle-aged woman: "Ego Integration and Patterns of Coniunctio". It was read to the first Congress of the International Association for Analytical Psychology in 1958. (It was published in *Current Trends in Analytical Psychology*, edited by myself, London 1958.)

Whereas all these papers deal with the case material and specific problems of practical psychotherapy, the next essay, "On the Question of Meaning in Psychotherapy", concerns itself with one of the most basic problems, that of the meaning of man's existence. Its point of departure is the question of the meaning of individual life, but it widens out into an examination of the cultural scene and the rôle analysis might play in the crisis of our civilization. The paper was read as the initial lecture in a cycle, "Towards the Meaning of our Time", arranged by the C.G. Jung Institute of Zürich in 1962. It was made sadly poignant by Jung's death a few months previously and written under the impression of this sad loss. It was originally published in *Psychotherapeutische Probleme*, the 17th volume of *Studien aus dem C.G. Jung-Institut Zürich*, in 1964. (An earlier English translation had appeared in *Spring 1963*, New York.)

A related subject is taken up in the next paper, "Personal Encounters with Jung". It is a personal account of my work and acquaintance with Jung over thirty years. It widens out into general considerations concerning the state of our civilization, its dangers and, hopefully, possible answers to them on the basis of Jung's contributions. It was written on the occasion of Jung's 100th birthday and read as the Centenary Lecture arranged by the Psychological Club, London. It was published in its Journal, *Harvest*, London, Number 21, 1975 as well as in the United States, Germany, France, and Italy.

A more theoretical approach is given in the next paper on "Analytical Psychology and the Principle of Complementarity". It was originally read to the Fourth Congress of the International Association for Analytical Psychology in 1968. It appears here in a revised form, omitting matters of internal policy of the Association. Starting from the vexed problem of frequent splits within every camp of depth psychology, it examines and tries to define the reasons for this. It was published in *The Analytic Process: Aims, Analysis, Training*, edited by Joseph B. Wheelwright, New York, 1971.

The last paper stands out both in length and in scope of its approach. In "Remembering and Forgetting" psychological, philosophical, mythological, and religious sources from various cultures and times are discussed from the angle of their relevance for the contrapuntal motif of remembering and forgetting. This leads also to the examination of such phenomena as *déjà vu*, the role of the neurotic symptom, the problem of egoless consciousness and other related subjects. The paper was read in a shortened form to the Second Panarion Conference held in Malibu, California, in 1976, (published here by permission of the Panarion Foundation), and again at two public meetings in 1978, organised jointly by the Association of Jungian Analysts (Alternative Training) and the Psychological Club, London. This paper is in many ways the synthesis of all other papers in this book and will, so I hope, represent a worthy conclusion to it.

Gerhard Adler,
London, January 1979

* * *

Note: The *Collected Works* of C.G. Jung are always referred to as "CW" with the number of the relevant volume following.
Jung's *Memories, Dreams, Reflections*, recorded and edited by Aniela Jaffé (New York and London, 1963) are referred to as *Memories*. Double page references pertain to the New York and London paperback editions respectively.

Basic Concepts of Analytical Psychology

It has often been remarked that Jung himself was the best advertisement for his ideas, that he represented the most convincing example of an integrated and individuated personality. It is indeed not easy to grasp the full message of Jung without having met him in the flesh. His maturity and serenity, his earthiness and sense of humour, the almost unbelievable range of his knowledge came so vividly across and formed such a colourful illustration of what he was teaching and aiming at, that a dimension of his theories seems to be missing without the embodiment of their practical fulfilment in his person. But, of course, it has to be accepted that to more and more people Jung's ideas are familiar only from his books, or, may be, from analysis with one of his direct or indirect pupils.

Perhaps it will help if I introduce my theoretical exposition with the narration of a personal experience right towards the end of Jung's life. It was the last time I saw Jung, a few months before his death. It was a Sunday morning and I had gone out to his Tower at Bollingen. His housekeeper told me to go upstairs to the study. I knocked at the door and went in. There the old man sat in his highly informal country clothes, at his writing desk, with a writing-pad in front of him and a fountain-pen in his hand. He had not heard me come in, and I stood, deeply moved, and almost embarrassed about my intrusion, for there, looking out over the lake of Zurich but clearly looking out very much further and deeper, he sat, completely unaware of my presence, intensely still and absolutely concentrated, utterly alone with himself and engrossed in his inner images — the picture of a sage completely absorbed in a world of his own, which yet is the infinite universe. This lasted only a few moments; then he noticed me; one could feel how he returned from far away, and the spell was broken. No doubt I had interrupted him, but he showed no trace of it, no sign of disturbance: there he was, at once deeply related to the other person and open to his presence.

I shall never forget the image of the sage contained in his inner universe, or the immediate return to the reality of the actual human situation. Both were the same man, and the interplay reveals a great deal about the nature of his genius.

It was indeed a long way which he had travelled to achieve such exceptional level of integration and it is this way which I shall now try to trace in its barest outlines and main stations. It started very early on in Jung's career with his doctoral dissertation *On the Psychology and Pathology of So-Called Occult Phenomena*. There already he had pointed out the *prospective nature of the unconscious* and what he called then "a highly developed intellectual activity of the unconscious."[1] His *Studies in Word Association* (1904-1907)[2] are generally well-known and thus I want to remind you here only of his discovery in that period of the *feeling-toned complexes*.

Since the word "complex" has entered common language in an often inaccurate way it may be useful to give Jung's own definition. He describes complexes as "psychic entities which are outside the control of the conscious mind. They have been split off from consciousness and lead a separate existence in the dark realm of the unconscious being at all times ready to hinder or reinforce the conscious functioning."[3]

Jung's discovery and experimental proof of complexes was an important step in putting the idea of the unconscious on firm ground. Freud was the first to recognize and acknowledge the importance of Jung's discovery and it made him eager to make Jung's acquaintance and win his co-operation. Jung sent Freud a copy of his *Studies in Word Association*, but Freud who had heard of Jung's researches was so impatient to know the results that he bought his own copy before Jung's had arrived.

Then there came the revolutionary publication in 1907 of *The Psychology of Dementia Praecox*[4] — as schizophrenia was called then — which showed the hidden or lost meaning behind the facade of apparently senseless behaviour and words. In consequence of this research Jung became the first psychiatrist to undertake the psychological treatment of schizophrenia, up to then thought unamenable to psychotherapy.

Jung's work on complexes and schizophrenia led to his *collaboration with Freud*. But it is worth remembering that Jung had already established himself with his writings, dealing with aspects of the unconscious before he met Freud and having made important contributions to the psychiatry of his time. In spite of various reservations, clearly expressed right from the beginning and right through the period of friendship, it was only with the publication of *Symbols of Transformation*, in 1912/13,[5] that the final break came. The correspondence between the two men, now available in print, gives a vivid picture of the vicissitudes of their relationship. Freud could not accept Jung's wider definition of the *nature of the libido* as not purely sexual and equally he could not accept Jung's idea of the *symbolic nature of incest*. The break was felt most seriously by both men. In spite of much bitterness engendered by it, Freud, towards the end of his life, could admit that Jung's departure had been a serious loss to himself and to the psychoanalytical movement; Jung, for his part, continued to honour and respect Freud's courageous pioneering in psychodynamics.

Yet the break with Freud led to an almost total isolation, forcing Jung to a completely new assessment and approach. We have only to read the chapter on "Confrontation with the Unconscious" in Jung's *Memories* to realize what a difficult and critical — but equally creative — time it was for him. A period of intense introspection laid the ground-work for most of Jung's later work. What had been called his heresy proved to be the foundation of a new creative approach, based on hitherto unknown empirical data. The break-through came with the *Psychological Types*[6] of 1921 in which Jung defined the two attitude-types of *introversion* and *extraversion*, with the subdivision of *four functional types*. This typology has often been misunderstood as trying to give a schematic cut-and-dried system of the psyche. In fact, however, the types are not static positions but point to the dynamic interplay of opposites by which any particular type of person is impelled by the need to complement this one-sidedness by the gradual assimilation of the missing adaptation.

Here then we find already the concept which would become

more and more central to Jung's approach; that of the *opposites in the psyche and their union*. This union is achieved in a process of integration which Jung termed the process of *individuation*. It can be defined as a constantly progressing assimilation of unconscious contents or as a constantly growing synthesis between the conscious mind and the unconscious. This presupposes a potentially *constructive function of the unconscious* by which it exerts a *compensatory effect* on the ego. In this way the unconscious functions are the constant regulators of the unconscious mind so that the psyche, consisting of conscious and unconscious, appears as a *self-regulating system*. Here the concept of homeostasis springs to mind. It has, however, to be understood that, in contradistinction to bodily homeostatic mechanisms, the psychic self-regulating system is progressive.[7] It is exactly these progressive acts of self-regulation which, in the ideal case, lead to the integrated and individuated personality whose centre Jung, in contradistinction to the *ego* as the centre of the conscious mind, has termed the *self*.

The concept of the psyche as a self-regulating system is based on Jung's theory of *psychic energy*.[8] Jung holds that the psyche cannot be understood from a purely causal point of view, but that this approach has to be complemented by a teleologic sense, according to which "causes are understood as means to an end",[9] in other words a point of view which interprets psychic facts as symbolic expressions of psychic developments.

In talking about the psyche as a self-regulating system we have to mention Jung's use and definition of the term "*symbol*." Here again, to this crucial psychological concept, Jung has made a distinctive and powerful contribution. To Freud symbols are the last irreducible translation of a dream-element into an image, e.g., stick or pistol for the male organ, or any form of container for the female organ. Jung regards this use of the term symbol as too static and points out that in Freud's instances we would do better to speak of signs. To Jung symbols express a reality so novel and complex as to transcend intellectual formulation: "When something is 'symbolic,' it means that a person divines its hidden, ungraspable nature and is trying desperately to capture in words the secret that eludes him."[10] Symbols thus represent psychic contents that cannot be expressed in any other form, and for this reason a true symbol is bound to contain a non-rational element that eludes conscious definition. This is exactly its function and explains the dynamic effect of any living symbol: by and in it unconscious contents are condensed and are forced into consciousness so that it acts as a *transformer of energy* and has a constructive integrative function. Here religious symbols spring to·mind as for instance those used in the mass and particularly that of the Cross.

The main form in which we experience symbols is as dream images. Thus, the *dream* itself fulfils a creative function in the process of integration. Far from regarding dreams as an illusory wish fulfilment or as "a pathological product",[11] Jung considers them as the entirely normal "spontaneous self-portrayal, in symbolic form, of the actual situation in the unconscious."[12] They have a *compensatory function* by revealing trends or states of which the conscious mind is unaware "either because of repression or through mere lack of realization."[13]

To give only one example: a highly intelligent man, an academic teacher in his mid-fifties, with a rather overdeveloped intellect and corresponding feeling-problem, sees in his dream a woman of exquisite beauty. While he is still admiringly looking at her she changes suddenly into a tall slender white lit candle of quite inexpressible beauty — if possible even more beautiful than the angelic woman. This graceful serenely-burning candle is perched on a tall stool, a kind of altar inspiring reverence and awe. — The woman here is an unequivocal symbol of what Jung has called the *anima*, the *femme inspiratrice*, the eternal feminine. But even she, in spite of her wonderful appearance, has to be divested of all possible personal implications and transformed into a symbol of spiritual illumination beyond rational human definition. This dream shows what Jung means by a symbol, just as it shows how *archetypes*, to which I shall turn presently, manifest themselves in the here and now of space and time.

The discussion of the process of individuation and of the symbol leads on to Jung's perhaps most important discovery, that of the *collective unconscious* and the *archetypal images* through which it manifests itself. This theory has undergone considerable development and modification in the course of time, as is only natural with a man whose creative working life extended over more than six decades. But its roots lie in Jung's earliest period.

As early as 1906, Jung made a decisive observation, which, however, at the time was too isolated and novel to be sufficiently understood and evaluated by him. One day a schizophrenic patient of his made him look out of a window and "showed" him the "*sun's phallus*" explaining that "if he moved his head from side to side the sun-phallus would move too, and that was the origin of the wind."[14] It was only some years later, in 1910, that Jung came across a book dealing with certain ancient mythological material in which he found to his astonishment a vision described in terms closely akin to the hallucination of the patient; it spoke of "a tube hanging down from the disc of the sun", which was "the origin of the ministering wind." Starting from this surprising parallelism Jung soon discovered that it was by no means fortuitous but that numerous mythological images turned up in dreams and phantasies of his patients who could not possibly have acquired knowledge of their existence.

These archaic *archetypal images* in their entirety form the impersonal substratum of the human psyche which Jung has termed the *collective unconscious*. This latter concept indicates that there are psychic contents in the unconscious of the individual which are not acquired during his personal life but are inherent in the specifically human psychic structure and organisation. Like anything else that enters consciousness they appear as ideas or images. Just as the *instincts* are typical *modes of action* so *archetypes* are typical *forms* of *behaviour*. Just as it is obvious that man has specific instinctive patterns, so he has also specific human patterns of behaviour. As such the archetypes act as unconscious "*regulators*" or "*dominants.*" Jung has expressed this in the analogy of "the axial system of a crystal which, as it were, preforms the crystaline structure in the mother liquid, although it has no material existence of its own ... The axial system determines only the stereometric structure but not the concrete form of the individual crystal", and similarly "the archetype in itself is empty and purely formal ...,"[15] a possibility of representation which is given *a priori*. It is thus not a fixed image as such that is innate in the psyche but the potentiality for certain types of images or actions.

It is noteworthy that in his last, unfinished work, *An Outline of Psychoanalysis*, written over twenty years after Jung had first formulated the concept of the collective unconscious, *Freud* came virtually to express the same idea. He wrote then "Dreams bring to light material which cannot have originated either from the dreamer's adult life or from his forgotten childhood. We are obliged to regard it as part of the archaic heritage which a child brings with him into the world, before any experience of his own, influenced by the experience of his ancestors. We find the counterpart of this phylogenetic material in the earliest human legends and in surviving customs."[16]

To return to the concept of the archetypes, it has to be understood that the archetype as such is a hypothesis, and that its existence can only be deduced from the archetypal images which appear in consciousness. Thus a clear distinction has to be made between the irrepresentable archetype and the archetypal image. I should like to give two examples of such archetypal images — one in human form, the other in a relatively abstract form.

"Mother", as the earliest and most influential figure, is the most decisive encounter in everybody's life, and accordingly produces a large amount of conscious and unconscious reactions and reaction formations. There is, however, more to it than just the reaction to the personal mother: in our psyche there is preformed, as it were, our expectation of the innumerable powerful aspects of the "maternal", which can very summarily be defined as "nature" and "matter", manifesting themselves as the life-giving and nourishing force on the one hand, but as the destructive and devouring force on the other. These various aspects are activated in our experience with the actual mother. They are brought to the surface in innumerable images which are all aspects of the underlying *mother-archetype*.

The child/mother-(and the child/parent)-relationship represents, therefore, always more than just the actual experience: in it and through it there are constellated instinctual patterns transcending the merely personal relationship and adding dimensions of intensity and meaning that are not given in the actual situation. The same can be said of all interpersonal encounters, among which the most powerful, apart from the parental experience and in part based on it, are the contrasexual experiences: man of woman and woman of man, and both constellate archetypal reactions transcending the merely personal experience. Jung has termed these two archetypes *animus* and *anima*, for which latter I have given an example in the previously mentioned dream.

Another, more abstract, archetypal image is linked up directly with the process of individuation. Jung found that this innate idea of individuation or psychic *wholeness* or totality found its symbolical expression in countless variations of the basic image of the circle (or square). In studying this phenomenon he discovered that circle and square are archetypal images of wholeness appearing in virtually every phase and culture of mankind.

Jung has dealt extensively with the symbol of the circle in his writings on the *mandala*.[17] Here I want to illustrate the appearance and function of this symbol by two short dreams. A woman patient of thirty-six dreamt the following dream before the start of her analysis: "I am in a semi-circular enclosed room and want to get into the corresponding room next door. I realize that I have to go right downstairs a long way and then up another way in order to get in." Here we have the symbolical expression for wholeness — the circular room to be completed — which can only be achieved after a descent into the unconscious. About three years later and towards the end of her analysis the same patient had another dream. She found herself in a round tower with four rooms arranged inside it like a Celtic cross. It is her own house, and she is immensely pleased with it. Here the combination of circle and square is a symbolic indication of the state of relative wholeness and centredness which she had achieved in her analytical work.

This *process of individuation* has in time become the focus and point of synthesis of all Jung's work. In view of a frequent misunderstanding of the concept of "individuation" as "individualism" I want to underline the fact that the two are not only not the same but diametrically opposed. Thus the process of individuation has been misrepresented as "an esoteric process which engages only the few."[18] As a matter of fact the process of individuation is an intrinsically normal process of growth and development leading to a mature and fully adjusted personality, attuned to both external and inner reality. Far from being esoteric or turning "the development of one's own personality into a kind of religion"[19] it leads to a fully responsible personality, willing and capable to play his role in the human community. Equally important, society consists of individuals and only when there are sufficient individuals in their own right, that is integrated and mature individuals, can society grow and blossom.

Jung's preoccupation with the process of individuation was also the reason behind his *alchemical studies*[20] to which he devoted so much of his later years. Here he found the historical link between early Christian Gnosticism and the modern discovery of the unconscious. In *alchemy* he saw the symbolical expression of inner experiences, aiming at psychic wholeness. He showed that a considerable part of alchemy was concerned not so much with pseudo-or-proto-chemistry but was a projection of unconscious psychic contents and images into the chemical process which thus served only as the projection screen for the adept's meditative realizations. In their experiments, the meditative side of which corresponded as a matter of fact to the process which Jung has called *active imagination*, these alchemists found their way of redemption, and the incorruptible *lapis*, the philosophers' stone, was the symbol of the archetype of the redeemer.

Alchemy, thus considered, has a profound relationship to the symbolism of dreams and to that of *religion*. Very early on in his work Jung had become convinced that the integrative function of the psyche was closely linked with religious images, and that in the symbols of religion mankind had at its disposal the creative answer to many of its problems. To mention only two of his essays, the one on the *Trinity* and the other one on the *Mass*[21] both showed the profound symbolical content of Christian concepts and rituals. It is equally borne out by his *Answer to Job*[22] which has aroused a great deal of controversy but to many, including myself, is his most personal and moving book. To Jung religion was of enormous significance for the health of the individual and the community alike, giving man's life meaning and direction and containing the answer to the syndrome of modern times, to *alienation*. Needless to say, it was not so much religion in any traditional or dogmatic sense that was Jung's concern as the individual's own and immediate experience of religious contents and images. To open and show the way to such experiences was the true purpose of his writings on religious subjects.

Here we have to mention also Jung's important theory of *synchronicity*.[23] By this concept he has provided a principle of explanation which complements an exclusively causal way of explanation. To quote Jung's own definition, it is "a coincidence in time of two or more causally unrelated events which have the same or a similar meaning."[24] By this new principle of explanation so far inexplicable phenomena become understandable, such as mantic methods — as e.g. that of the Chinese oracle of the *I Ching* — telepathy, clairvoyance, or other manifestations of ESP; equally, other strange phenomena, so far explained — or explained away — as "chance" or "accident" gain a new meaning. Another field where this concept can provide new insights is the relationship between body and soul, in that the interdependence of psychic and physical processes in the living organism can be understood not so much as a causal relationship but as a synchronistic phenomenon.

Synchronistic phenomena, and in particular those of ESP, convinced Jung of the existence of a transcendental *"absolute knowledge"*, independent of the senses.[25] It is transcendental in that "synchronicity postulates a meaning which is a priori in relation to human consciousness and *apparently exists outside man"* (my italics).[26] It is needless to stress the importance of such conclusions for religious thought.

Researches like these or into alchemy and *religious symbolism* have led to the frequent misunderstanding of Jung as a mystic, and he has often been attacked for lack of clarity and vagueness. Jung was fully aware of this problem. He expressed it once to me when I had mentioned certain points in his *Psychological Types* which did not seem clear enough. He said: "People complain that my findings are too intuitive, but they don't understand what I have to try and do. I have to catch the reflections of the primeval fire in mirrors I put around it; and of course, the mirrors are not always a perfect fit at the corners."

From his remark we can understand that, what has been regarded as inexactitude, springs from his familiarity with irrational and *numinous processes* inaccessible to most people and evading strictly rational definition. In the same way the symbol has, as we have seen, an irrational aspect precisely because it deals with experiences beyond purely logical description. Jung's attitude has to be understood as comprising both rational and irrational facts and thus initiating a completely new scientific approach.

Jung himself has made a revealing comment on this problem of "inexactitude." In a letter of 1952 he wrote: "The language I speak must be ambiguous, must have two meanings in order to be fair to the dual aspect of our psychic nature. I strive quite consciously and deliberately for ambiguity of expression because it is superior to unequivocality and reflects the nature of life. My whole temperament inclines me to be very unequivocal indeed. That is not difficult, but it would be at the cost of truth. I purposely allow all the overtones and undertones to be heard, partly because they are there anyway, and partly because they give a fuller picture of reality. Unequivocality makes sense only in establishing facts but not in interpreting them."[27][n1]

An interesting comment on the power and effect of Jung's concepts has often been provided to me by people remarking that although they could not really follow Jung's ideas they felt deeply moved by them; or, in one extreme case, when a woman patient said: "I hardly understood a word of what I read, but I knew I had to go to Zürich." And she did. Remarks like those make it evident that Jung's words, although they are somehow equivocal, speak to the unconscious of people, to their guts, and stir much deeper layers than those of reason.

Jung was strongly attracted to the rejected areas of the psyche. His interest in the border areas of the human psyche and their numinous contents did not spring from a mystical inclination but from insatiable curiosity and intellectual honesty. It led him to explore phenomena which other people carefully avoided as unfashionable or "unscientific." He had to study these and other subjects simply because they existed and manifested vital aspects of the psyche. His discursive, intuitive style and *open system* are the direct results of an interest much wider than in the usual fields of research. He refused to develop a closed system exactly because he was open to every human phenomenon.

This attitude has, however, the most decisive consequences. One of its most important results is the significance it lends to a deeper and wider understanding of human history, as well as of religious and artistic creativity. It is in these fields that the concept of the collective unconscious and of the archetypes shows its general significance and can lead to new creative insights. All human behaviour is lastly dependent on and directed by arche-typal forces, and the archetype mediates between the unconscious foundations of the human psyche and the conscious mind. It is from this angle that Jung's later researches have to be under-stood. In them he considered individuation not merely from the point of view of the individual but as a process of the development of human consciousness in general. But all these researches even where they concern themselves with highly complex collective symbolism lead in the end back to the part the individual has to play in the growth of human consciousness.

In particular Jung's concepts of the *shadow* and of the mechanism of *projection* — so important for the psychology of the individual — can be most fruitfully applied to man's social and political activities. We are all only too aware of the deep split running through the world as well as through our own body politic. Jung was deeply concerned about these splits — witness his *"Undiscovered Self"* (which in German carried the much more indicative title "Present and Future"). His whole work convinced him that only the realization and withdrawal of such projections, accompanied by the growing consciousness of individuals relating to the archetypal foundations of the human psyche, could lessen the tension and lead us out of the critical situation of our time.

As far as *religious* or *artistic creativeness* is concerned they have to be understood as the ego's — successful or unsuccessful — endeavours to get in touch with the eternal images and to reformulate them through the medium of consciousness. Here the idea of the archetypes as regulators or dominants has proved itself highly relevant for the general human situation. Jung's essays on such divers subjects as Picasso or James Joyce,[29] on the symbolism of the Trinity or the Mass, or on the political situation of our time bear witness to the importance of these findings which far transcend the narrow field of medical psychology. His researches amount to the realization that the external world cannot be understood without reference to the inner world of the eternal archetypal images, indeed, that all the elements of external knowledge rest on these psychic images.

In a more general way this means that the split between "outside" and "inside" has become reconciled and that the connection between subject and object has been reconstituted. Here true religion can play a decisive role, and that explains Jung's intense interest in religion. Religion, as has been mentioned, to him was a tremendously individual concern: all collective formulations were only preliminary, and genuine *personal experience* of the eternal images was the final aim. Thus he has been attacked by both religious and materialistic thinkers; to the first he appeared as an iconoclast, to the latter as a mystic. But his real concern was with man's psychic health and balance which could only be restored by an individually responsible connection with and commitment to the realm of eternal images. Thus Jung has restored the dignity of the individual as the creative nuclear element of human civilization and created the basis for a new ethics, based on the authenticity and commitment of the individual.

Perhaps Jung's significance is best expressed in the short words formulated by the proverbially sober Swiss in the document given to him in 1955, when they made him an honorary doctor of science of the Federal Technical University of Zürich:

To the rediscoverer of the totality and polarity of the human psyche and its striving for unity —

To the diagnostician of the crisis of man in the age of science and technique —

To the interpreter of the primeval symbolism and of the individuation process of mankind ...

REFERENCES

1 CW 1, par. 148
2 In CW 2
3 CW 6, par. 923
4 In CW 3
5 Now in revised form in CW 5
6 CW 6
7 Michael Fordham, *The Objective Psyche* (London, 1958), p. 82
8 cf. CW 8
9 Ibid., par. 43
10 CW 15, par. 185
11 Sigmund Freud, "New Introductory Lecture on Psychoanalysis", Stand. Ed., Vol. 22
12 CW 8, par. 505
13 Ibid., par. 477
14 CW 8, par. 317f.
15 CW 9.1, par. 155
16 Freud, "An Outline of Psychoanalysis", Stand. Ed., Vol. 23
17 cf. e.g. CW 9.1
18 Anthony Storr, *Jung*, (London, 1973), p. 81
19 Ibid., p. 90
20 cf. CW 12, 13, 14
21 In CW 11
22 Ibid.
23 In CW 8
24 Ibid., par. 849
25 Ibid., par. 948
26 Ibid., par. 942
27 *Letters*, Vol. 2, p. 70
28 In CW 10
29 Both in CW 15

NOTES

1 cf. also below "Depth Psychology and the Principle of Complementarity", p. 109

The Dynamics of the Self

One of the most important questions for practical psychotherapy concerned the nature of the power, the *dynamis*, operative in and behind the process of healing. "Healing" means growing self-realization. But what is this "self-realization"? It is here that C. G. Jung has made probably the weightiest contribution to our understanding of the curative process, and of psychic processes in general. He has shown what this self-realization is, namely the realization of the self, that is of a personality which is far more comprehensive than our conscious personality, the ego. This "self" comprises both the conscious and the unconscious, the unconscious here understood in the Jungian sense, as the "non-ego", the collective unconscious, "the broad basis of an inherited and universal psychic disposition which is as such unconscious, and upon which our personal and conscious psyche rests"[1]; it is "the hypothetical point between conscious and unconscious"[2], a new centre of gravity for the personality, representing the synthesis of the conscious and the unconscious psyche. Hence the self is not only the foundation and ground of the personality but at the same time its fulfilment in an all-embracing and meaningful relation to the world. So understood, the individual human being stands there as a special instance of the transpersonal creative principle, but on the other hand this very principle needs him for its specific realization. The process through which this self-realization occurs is called by Jung the process of individuation.

The purpose of this essay is to provide material from case-histories in order to shed light on this problem of the self and its realization in the individuation process. Two aspects of the self will have to be considered. In the first place the self, as the new centre of gravity and the synthesis of conscious and unconscious (of ego and non-ego), is the goal of the individuation process; but as we shall try to show it is at the same time the *dynamis* behind this same process, the power which sets it in motion and which seeks to assert and realize itself therein, despite all the twists and turns of empirical existence.

It is inherent in Jung's concept of the self that it is active, and thus observable, through the whole of our life. Thus Jung said in his essay on "Transformation Symbolism in the Mass": "Human nature has an invincible dread of becoming more conscious of itself. What nevertheless drives us to it is the self … Conscious realization … is in one sense an act of the ego's will, but in another sense it is a spontaneous manifestation of the self, which was always there."[3]

As I am going to use as one of my two illustrations for the dynamics of the self the case of a girl of 5, I should like to acknowledge also Dr. Michael Fordham's contribution which he made in his paper on "Integration and Disintegration and early Ego Development" in 1947.[4] In this paper he published, as far as I know, the first explicit observation of the emergence of the self in childhood. He says: "In this paper I put forward the thesis that the very small child can, and frequently does, experience an image of himself as an integrated whole, not merely as an ego, but also as a self … ", and he has given convincing material for this thesis in his paper.

In its relative realization in the individuation process, the self is always a result of the action of the non-ego upon the ego. We might say that "normality", as the most complete synthesis, is dependent upon the degree of "permeability" to the images of the collective unconscious, the so-called archetypes (which belong to the layer of the non-ego), and upon their assimilation by the ego. In this process the centre of gravity of the personality shifts more and more away from the sphere of the ego to that of the non-ego. Its final aim is that of the integration of the unconscious into consciousness, or, more correctly, of "the assimilation of the ego to a wider personality".[5] This individuation process — a steady integration of the emergent archetypal material — is, however, only possible where an already developed and coherent ego can act as a receptive organ. Among children, therefore, the process of psychic growth has as its first task the gradual development of the ego from its original condition of imprisonment in, so to speak, a mythical pre-conscious stage. The remark of a five-year-old child, reported by Jean Piaget, is relevant here: "Moi je suis dans le rêve, le rêve n'est pas dans ma tête."[6][n1]

Now the important point here is that although in childhood (up to about the time of puberty) the crucial task is the development of the ego and consequently of a coherent field of consciousness, this task seems nevertheless to be directed by the self. In other words the self, acting as dynamis and eidos, drives the fragmentary ego-consciousness progressively away from the non-ego, the collective unconscious, we might well say in order to mould it into an organ capable of perceiving itself, thus turning ego-consciousness into self-consciousness, i.e. consciousness of the self. Here we can observe the law governing all psychic processes: the self-regulation of the psyche. Where, as in the latter stages of life, the personality needs to limit the ego-sphere in favour of the non-ego sphere (that is to say, where the individual is faced with the task of adapting to the "interior world" of the archetypes), the non-ego becomes so charged with energy that the ego has to retire in order to make room for the higher energy of the non-ego. The situation is reversed in childhood: here the non-ego has the upper hand at first, and the self charges the ego-function with sufficient energy for it to establish itself against the non-ego, so that it can fulfil the demands of adaptation to the outer world. In both cases the self operates as an image of potential wholeness[7] behind the psychic processes and bends them towards the realization of this wholeness, which appears as the synthesis of ego and non-ego, of conscious and unconscious, of the inner and outer worlds.[8]

The most important figures in any childhood are those of the parents. Jung has emphasized the salient fact that the real significance of the parents depends not only on their personal, concrete reality but first and foremost on the archetypal configuration which is activated by their personal existence.[9] It is against the overpowering energy of these archetypal images that the fragmentary ego of the child has to assert itself.[10] In normal cases, where the personal parents do not, through their own excessive unconsciousness and the resultant projections upon the child, hinder the growth and integration of its ego, the detachment from the archetypal substratum takes place without abnormal conflicts. The child gradually disengages itself from its "dream", becoming more and more capable of perceiving it as

the ego wakens and grows coherent: Very revealing in this
connection is the remark of an eight-year-old boy, who said to his
mother: "The questions I want to talk about I keep in my head,
and those I don't want to talk about I keep in my tummy".
Already there is a differential perception as between the ego
(head) and the non-ego (tummy).

Often the meaning of this normal process of development can
best be seen by contrasting it with a pathological disturbance.
The picture now to be described (Fig. 1) was painted by a
five-year-old girl who, about a year before, came for psycho-
therapeutic treatment on account of chronic, and as the treatment showed, psychogenic constipation.[n2] Although her
parents were "deeply unhappy" about the child's difficulties, the
treatment very soon proved how much they themselves were
responsible for these difficulties. The constipation had set in
immediately after the child's birth, and none of the unending
medical and medicinal remedies had shown itself of the least
avail. The child's constipation had turned into the main topic of
conversation and become the mainstay of relations between the
parents, but on the other hand there was obviously an almost
complete lack of genuine love and adult understanding of the
child. The chief problem lay, as might be expected, with the
mother. She was an overbearing character, eaten up with
resentment against her feminine role. The father was a weakling,
under the thumb of his wife, a rigid and narrow person. After
the birth of the child the mother had been overtaken by a severe
depression and refused to feed the child herself; in every way she
had pushed the child from her. When the little girl, then little
more than four years old, came along for treatment, she was
quite incapable of showing or of accepting any feelings at all, so
much so that she was obviously making desperate efforts to hide
her emotional reactions, and of this her constipation was only the
physical expression. It is notorious that nothing is more catastro-
phic for children than the loss of the mother or her love, which is
the very soil they grow in; and the mother's repudiation had
made it impossible for the child to take root in this natural soil
and thus to develop her emotional life. During treatment it soon
became clear how much, despite her desperate defence against

Fig. 1.

Fig. 2.

all feelings (which was really only the result of the trauma of repudiation), the little girl longed in her heart for sympathy and understanding. In the end she could develop this side of her personality in the transference relationship to the doctor, even though her strong resistance made it extremely difficult to break the barriers down. The picture she painted was done after a year's treatment. She herself explained it as follows: "A wicked man (left) and a wicked woman (right) want to hurt the good fairy (in the circle). They want to see how she does her 'big business'; that is why she stops in the circle where they cannot reach her."

It is evident that the child feels threatened by her parents. She feels that "they want to see how she does her big business"; in other words she feels how the curiosity of the parents tries to intrude into her intimate personality. This parental curiosity expresses the lack of consciousness and discrimination in them. The legitimate frontiers of the mutual personalities are broken down by the parental projections and by a process of unconscious identification on their part. The very fact that the constipation of the child plays such an important part in the life of the parents shows how they live a kind of vicarious existence in their identification with the girl.

Against this interference the child has to protect herself. The painting shown here is only one among many which contain the motif of the protecting circle or space (the *temenos*). The *temenos* is in this case the magic circle into which the child can withdraw so as not to be overpowered by the unconscious of the parents. (In another drawing (Fig. 2), done a fortnight before the first one, the motif of the "magic flower" appeared, symbolizing her individuality; it shows a big blue flower with a centre, menaced by two figures, a giant and a witch-like woman. It is interesting to see how in this first picture there is no clear demarcation-line against the outside world; the *temenos* round the flower and its centre is still lacking.)

The protective circle is what Jung has described as *mandala*. Mandalas in the East are constructed and used as *yantras*, as instruments of contemplation. Jung reports that the Abbot of a lamaistic monastery explained to him the function of a mandala as that of an inner synthesizing image which has to be constructed by imagination whenever the psychic balance is disturbed.[11] In the analysis of western people mandalas occur frequently as compensation to a conscious situation full of conflicts and disturbance. They represent a spontaneous attempt on the side of the unconscious at creating a centre of personality, thus leading over from a state of dissociation and disorientation to a new order.[12]

The usual structure of a mandala is that of a circle (or square) with a centre. In the East the centre contains a figure of high religious value, as e.g. Shiva, Buddha, etc. It is the essential object and aim of contemplation. In modern western mandalas we find mostly instead of some traditional and conventional object of meditation an individual object of particular significance. The circle around this centre fulfils a double function: it acts as protection against intrusion and interference, and at the same time it holds the content of the circle together and prevents its dissipation into the environment. In other words, the circle divides and defines the area inside as a coherent and numinous sphere, thus creating a *temenos*, a holy inviolable area. (Cf. the function of the *sulcus primigenius* in the foundation of ancient settlements.)

Such a *temenos* has been produced by the girl in her painting. Inside she puts her own highest value, symbolized by the good fairy. The good fairy has magic power of a helpful and constructive character; she represents the child's anticipation of her own undisturbed and creative personality. This highest value has to be protected from the attack of the parental imagos; thus the child draws the circle round it inside which this highest value is safe from their destructive influence. At the same time the *temenos* fulfils its function of container; it acts as a kind of magic eggshell, but alive and full of vital power. It is a symbolical womb, the *krater* of alchemy, the *vas bene clausum* inside which the transmutation takes place.

The circle, the roundness, symbolizes wholeness and integration, and as such the self. Inside this circle of the self the child experiences her own intact personality. This experience is at that particular stage of development identical with the experience of the ego. To the child the fact and power of this new ego-experience with the completely new possibilities which it opens up, must indeed appear as magic, and the good fairy would be a most adequate symbol for this. The drawing is an elaboration of the well-known scheme of the circle with the dot in the centre, where the circle would be the protective *temenos* inside which the ego can be established. Fordham, who has given several instances of this in his above-mentioned paper, says: "If we regard the circle as the self, then we can grasp that it represents an essential precondition for the formation of the organized ego", a statement with which I am in full agreement.

To sum up, we might describe the situation as follows: the circle in the drawing is the symbol of the self, of integration. The good fairy represents the highest value of the child in her particular situation; it symbolizes the ego. It is therefore in the sphere of the self that the child feels safe from the destructive influence of the parental imagos, and it is inside this *temenos* that the child can fulfil the task that befits her particular situation in the life-long process of individuation; it is here that she can develop her ego undisturbed.

The self then, symbolized by the circle, is the symbolical matrix which the child, under the stress of the situation and aided by the psychotherapist, has won for herself in place of the natural matrix — or rather which, more accurately speaking, has offered itself to her in this early crisis of her life. For the child the parents are the natural carriers of the projection of the unconscious self; but when, as in the case we have described, the actual parents cannot meet the needs of the projection, the self must become constellated and effective in another way. This is what is anticipated in the painting. And, in fact, a noticeable improvement in the child's condition set in soon afterwards, leading to the complete disappearance of the symptoms. The physical as well as the emotional constipation vanished, and the child became an open-hearted and friendly girl quite capable of displaying her feelings freely.

The decisive factor is the role of the self which, though, of course, the child was wholly unconscious of it, acts as the real driving force behind development and the cure. In accordance with the early phase of the child's life, when the development of the ego out of the non-ego and away from the fascination of its mythical images constitutes the specific task of the life-process, the self protects the ego and assists its formation. We would expect that in a later phase of life, when ego-formation is complete, a corresponding process would be initiated in the direction of the non-ego. Analysis of people in the second half of life, unless of course they are suffering from severe pathological disturbances, does in fact prove the validity of this supposition. For this I want in the following to give one typical example.

It concerns the dream of a woman of forty, married, professionally independent and with no special neurotic problems. The dream occurred six weeks after the beginning of analysis and is here given in slightly abbreviated form:

> My friends... have had a child... I am looking forward to seeing him. But on my first visit to them they do not show him to me. I come a second time... This time the father is alone and takes me into the room where I shall find the child. I experience a great shock, for the child is *not* beautiful: he is grey from head to foot; he is completely encased in a layer of dull grey metal, suggesting lead. He is not so young as I had expected: he is sitting up in his cot, and he tries with a silver spoon to remove this layer of metal. He had succeeded at one spot, near the navel, but he had also hurt himself in the process and some blood is appearing. I am filled with horror. I think that it is a terrible affliction for the parents to have such a child... But suddenly I feel that my own face is covered with the same grey lead, and I am terrified... I think: "O *why* has it happened? I was so happy before that! And how shall I be able to show myself to my husband? From now on I shall have to be veiled." I feel as if I could not breathe freely, and this feeling of oppression wakes me up.

The symbolism of this dream is so rich and varied that we shall have to confine ourselves to mere hints. The child in its leaden encasement is the main theme of the dream, and it is also especially relevant to our subject. The symbolical meaning of the

child has been enlarged upon by Jung.[13] Its central meaning is
that of potential futurity. The child is "an anticipation of future
developments", and "in the individuation process it anticipates
the figure that comes from the synthesis of conscious and
unconscious elements in the personality". As such it is "a symbol
which unites the opposites; a mediator, bringer of healing, that
is, one who makes whole.[14] It is a symbol of wholeness, in other
words, of the self.

For further understanding of the dream we must draw upon
the symbolism of alchemy, as described by Jung in his fundamental work, *Psychology and Alchemy*. He has shown that the
esoteric theme of alchemy is the psychic process of individuation.
This is represented in alchemy as the liberation of the *lapis*, the
philosophers' stone, from the embrace of gross matter, the *prima
materia*, the lapis being a symbol of what modern psychology
would call the self. For this reason the *prima materia* is on the
other hand the "black, magically fertile earth" in which the lapis
grows like the grain of wheat; the *prima materia* is the "precondition and first stage" of the lapis.

The dream is clearly concerned with the birth of this self, but
not so much with a physical birth — for in this concrete sense the
child had been born already — as with a second, symbolical
birth, represented as the liberation from the "leaden uterus".
Lead is the *prima materia par excellence* of the alchemists. It is
heavy, grey, poisonous, insignificant-looking and of little worth.
(Thus the motifs of "miraculous birth" and of the "insignificant
beginning", which Jung describes as pertaining to the symbolism
of the "divine child",[15] both make their appearance here.) As
to the further symbolism of the dream, the magic child with the
appellatives *filius philosophorum* or *filius macrocosmi* is one of
the commonest designations for the lapis. What the dream is
portraying in symbolical form is the painful (cf. the blood) birth
of the self, the *opus magnum* of the alchemists, the "uncovering"
and freeing of wholeness from the gross matter of the merely
collective man, living in a state of unconscious identification. In
every mythology one of the mightiest feats of the hero and
redeemer, who so often appears as the child, is "to overcome the
monster of darkness",[16] i.e. of unconsciousness enveloping
man.

The dreamer herself commented on the dream as follows: "The reluctance of the mother to show the child to me, as opposed to the willingness of the father, seems to express my own reluctance, as a woman, to accept any markedly spiritual development as opposed to simple happiness on a more natural level. Hence the feeling of isolation at the end of the dream, which immediately on waking up suggested the verse: 'He was despised and rejected of all men, a man of sorrows and acquainted with grief'." Here the identity of the child', as a symbol of the dreamer's spiritual development, the self, with the lapis is very clearly expressed. It is "the stone which the builders rejected and which became the head of the corner". Actually, the quotation comes from the text of Handel's *Messiah*. It was the only source which the dreamer remembered. All the more surprising and convincing, therefore, is the original context in Isaiah 53: 2-3: "He hath no form nor comeliness; and when we shall see him, there is no beauty that we should desire in him. He is despised and rejected of men: a man of sorrows and acquainted with grief: and we hid as it were our faces from him; he was despised, and we esteemed him not." The parallels to our dream are even more obvious in this original text and quite unmistakable.

Significantly enough, the dream-child is the child of some friends who, as she said, first introduced her to Jung's analytical psychology and its ideas; so it was indirectly through them that she took the decisive step of being analysed. These friends are as it were the symbolical parents (cf. the English expression "godparents" and its Swiss equivalent "Götti") of her inner development. The sight of the child imparts the leaden sheath to her own "personal" face, thus indicating her inner identity with the child. Her unhappiness at being thrown back upon her own resources, her alienation from the "natural" life of a married woman, are the necessary pre-condition and concomitant of individuation: "The self ... [is the] 'absolutely other' ... Only because of this psychic 'otherness' is consciousness possible at all. Identity does not make consciousness possible; it is only separation, detachment, and agonizing confrontation through opposition that produces consciousness and insight".[17] Finally the "silver-spoon", the tool with which the child begins his work of liberation, can be illuminated by reference to the silver of the alchemists: it was the raw material for the so-called "sophical quicksilver" (not to be confused with Hg!), known as the "quicksilver of the philosophers" or the "quintessence of metals", in which capacity it was used in preparing the stone.[18] At the same time the first stage of the *opus alchymicum*, the immediate goal of the process and outcome of the *nigredo* (the initial stage of "blackness"), is the *albedo* or "whiteness" which was regarded as the silver or moon state.[19]

It is instructive to see how the two manifestations of the unconscious we have mentioned — the child's painting and the middle-aged woman's dream — tend in opposite directions and yet stand for the same process of individuation. In the case of the child it is the ego that is sheltered in the self and has to be born out of it; here the unconscious process of individuation, striving towards future wholeness, is incorporated in the ego, the representative of consciousness. The stress lies, therefore, on the hard-pressed differentiation of the ego from its identity with the parents who, as archetypal images, symbolize the non-ego. On the other hand, in the case of the grown-up woman who has fulfilled the demands of the ego, the process is reversed. Here the non-ego comes more and more to the forefront so that the self, the "divine child", may be born out of the *massa informis*, the "darkness of matter" belonging to the empirical, limited personality. Here the stress lies on the painful differentiation of the non-ego from the preliminary and incomplete ego-existence (which explains why, in this phase of life, besides typical birth dreams there occur so many death dreams pointing in the direction of the "Stirb und Werde", "die and become").

In both cases, that of the girl of five and that of the grown-up woman, we can find a clear hint at what activated the emergence of the image of the self: it is a state of need, of an inner crisis which cannot be answered along the usual, as it were, "natural" line of development. It is one of the most impressive experiences of the psychotherapist to see how the self always emerges out of a situation which is strictly speaking "un-natural", i.e. where the straightforward, biological-collective development has come to an impasse and needs a completely new and often utterly unexpected answer. The more one sees of such crises and the solutions arising out of this state of emergency, the more one comprehends the fundamental truth of the alchemical sentence: *Opus contra naturam est*, "the 'work' is against nature".

The state of "nature" represented to the alchemists a state in which "spirit" — the "philosophers' stone" — was completely hidden and imprisoned in base matter; it needed a transmutation of this "natural" state to free the lapis out of the so-called prima materia. Their *opus contra naturam* thus expresses the fact that our psyche has the unique capacity to change collective and biological drives into individual and spiritual drives of a higher and, as it were, "unnatural" order.[n3] To the alchemists who were still largely — though not wholly — unconscious of their inner psychic processes, these were projected into matter.[n4] This projection produced an unconscious identity between the psyche of the alchemist and "spirit" which he perceived as imprisoned in matter. In other words, what the alchemists described as their *opus magnum*, the freeing of the lapis from the bonds of physis, can be described in modern psychological language as the withdrawal of projections and identifications by which the conscious and integrated personality emerges out of its pre-conscious state.

What we call "ego-consciousness" is strictly speaking still largely a state of identification and projection. On the level of so-called ego-consciousness we are still to a considerable degree identified with the internal conditionings by instinctive drives and impulses on the one hand and with the unconscious and collective trends of our environment on the other. The state of ego-consciousness could from this angle just as well be described as a state of preliminary collective consciousness. As Jung has put it: "Natural man is not a self — he is the mass and a particle in the mass, collective to such a degree that he is not even sure of his own ego."[20] It seems, therefore, to need a particularly stringent situation to force our "natural" psychology out of its collective direction towards the emergence and acceptance of its underlying drive towards individuation. This road can be described in Jung's words as "actualizing those contents of the unconscious which are outside nature, i.e., not a datum of our empirical world, and therefore an *a priori* of archetypal character".[21]

The kind of psychological situation which produces unexpected solutions in the direction of individuation is well illustrated by
another dream of the woman mentioned above. She dreamt this
dream two months after the dream of the leaden child. It was as
follows:

> I am in a lavatory with a little girl of about seven. I am about
> to sit down when the little girl lowers the wooden lid of the seat,
> thus preventing me from using it. An immediate reflex sets in,
> and instead of evacuating the excrements in the normal way I
> find myself vomiting them with extreme disgust.

Here the release and satisfaction of a natural urge is interrupted by a child of seven and leads to an "un-natural" solution of an
emergency situation. With regard to the girl of seven in the
dream, the dreamer relates that her father left her mother for
good when she was seven years old. This leads us to the conclusion
that the loss of her father produced a crisis which on the one hand
interfered with her natural development and which on the other
hand had to be solved by a quite new and unexpected answer.
This answer is given as the defecation through the mouth.

We would commit a fundamental mistake if we tried to
interpret this dream-content of defecation in a reductive way as
merely representing a problem of infantile anal or oral sexuality.
The dream is dreamt by a relatively well-integrated person, with
a normal adaptation to life and with normal sexuality. Moreover,
her previous dream of the child in the lead uterus has shown us
what her real quest is: that of individuation. We have, therefore,
to interpret the dream from a synthetic-constructive point of view,
and not from an analytical-reductive one. In other words, we
have to try and understand the symbolical meaning of the
defecation through the mouth.

What, first of all, are the facts of the dream? A normal need
for defecation is interfered with by a girl of seven, and this
interference leads to an abnormal release. The process of defecation represents normal purification, normal removal of waste
material. But something has apparently happened that inhibits
this normal process of life. For the dreamer's association it is clear

what it is: it is the disappearance of the father, which has produced such a severe trauma that the normal organic functioning is interrupted. As there is no such organic symptom in actual fact, we have to understand it symbolically: the psychic life is under such an immense strain and tension that the normal "psychic metabolism" is profoundly disturbed. One could say that, if this disturbance were to stop the removal of waste material, a deep neurosis would be the result. As a matter of fact, this is exactly the state of affairs as we have seen it happening in the case of the girl of five who reacted to the trauma of lacking mother-love by concretely stopping defecation and thus expressing symbolically her refusal to relate to her environment.

But in the dream of the adult woman something else and quite unforeseeable happens. Through the trauma a new mode of purification is produced — an "un-natural" one, or, as we may interpret it, a symbolical and individual one. Defecation stands for the lower functions, the lower biological processes in general. Their satisfaction would lead to a biologically and collectively satisfactory adjustment, to a so-called normal development. Stoppage, on the other hand, would lead to a neurosis. In our case a third mode of reaction is shown: the mouth instead of the anus serves as channel of exteriorization, or, in the literal and original meaning of the word, as channel of "expression".

What is exteriorized through the mouth, is "expressed" by means of it, has symbolically to be understood as "word", as "logos". In other words the situation of emergency, of need, produced by the traumatic situation of the child, has called forth a spiritualization of her original biological collective need. We must not forget that the dream is dreamt by an adult and that in the dream it is the adult — and not the child of seven — who is inhibited in her normal release. Therefore, we can say that the shock of the father's disappearance has at the time produced an impulse towards spiritualization, towards individuation, which now, in and through analysis, and moreover, in a phase of life which tends towards this very individuation, has broken through and reasserted itself.

It is hardly necessary to say that such a situation is fraught with danger, and that every challenge of this kind which forces a child — or for all that, an adult — to deviate from the natural, collective line, may lead to the most serious disturbance. But this is exactly what we want to show; that the very situation which might be instrumental in creating the most serious disturbance of balance, is also the one which might, on the other hand, forcefully open the gateway to individuation. This is indeed the basic ambivalence of each such crisis of life. We find the same ambivalence expressed in the use made by alchemy of the symbol of faeces and urine. The old saying: *Inter faeces et urinas nascimur* — between excrements and urine are we born — had been raised by the adepts into the realization of the *enantiodromeia*[n5] inherent in the very lowness of matter. One of the frequent symbols used by the alchemists for the lapis is that of faeces or of urine. The *prima materia*, the matter out of which the lapis will be developed, is to be found everywhere, and thus also in the human body; it is cheap and vile and can be found "in the streets", and even in excrement: *In stercore invenitur*.[22]

Thus it is just the situation of need and despair, of a seemingly hopeless crisis, of one's own deepest humiliation which so often forces an unexpected and individual answer on us. Again this is expressed by the alchemists under the symbol of the nigredo, of the darkness of the soul. It is in this and out of this darkness that the lapis, the self-germ is so often born.

What is going to happen to the girl of five whose case we discussed above, we cannot say. All we know from her drawing is that the self has become manifest as an active force in her life out of her crisis and loneliness. But the case of the grown-up woman shows a surprising parallelism, and as we know at least a few facts of her later development, we can venture to draw a few conclusions about the effect produced by her early crisis, her early nigredo. To be wounded means also to have the healing power activated in us; or might we possibly say that without being wounded one would never meet just this healing power? Might we even go as far as to say: the very purpose of being wounded is to be shown the healing power in us?[n6]

However this may be, the conclusion which is forced upon us if we try to sum our two cases up, is this: that the self is the decisive force behind the psychic process. The child's fear may incline it to run away from the necessity of developing an ego, just as the adult's fear may cause him to shrink from its necessary sacrifice; but in either case the point of reference is the self. A positive relationship with it is established where the psychic process tends towards progression, that is, its acceptance and realization, a negative where it tends towards regression, rejection and stagnation. In its double aspect as pre-existent image of the total personality and as impulse towards its own realization the self holds the key to the process of individuation.

REFERENCES

1 CW 7, par. 234
2 CW 13, par. 67
3 CW 11, par. 400
4 Michael Fordham, in: *The Nervous Child*, 6, no. 3, 1928
5 CW 8, par. 557
6 Jean Piaget, "La pensée symbolique et la pensée de l'enfant", *Arch. Psychol.*, Genève, 18
7 Erich Neumann has described this process as "introversion"; cf. his *The Origin and History of Consciousness*, (New York/London 1954)
8 cf. Gerhard Adler, *Studies in Analytical Psychology*, (2nd ed. London 1966, New York 1967), pp. 167ff.
9 CW 9,1
10 Gerhard Adler, op. cit., p. 129 and ill. 12
11 CW 12, par. 123
12 CW 9, 1, par. 710
13 "The Psychology of the Child Archetype", CW 9,1
14 Ibid., par. 278
15 Ibid., par. 282
16 Ibid., par. 284
17 Ibid., par. 289
18 John Read, *Prelude to Chemistry*, (London, 1939), p. 132; CW 14, par. 719
19 CW 12, par. 334; CW 14, passim.
20 CW 12, par. 104
21 Ibid., par. 400
22 Ibid., note 46 to par. 421

NOTES

1 In this connection it is interesting to note the great role that the skin seems to play in the life of the newborn infant. Playing with its own body, it learns its demarcation from the surrounding world. It is as though the skin, the "four walls" or "circle" of the body formed a magic circle, a sort of "primordial mandala" marking off an "ego sphere" and a "non-ego sphere", and within which the ego experiences itself sensorially. Cf. Neumann, *The Child*, (New York, 1973), p. 111: "The child's unitary body-feeling is the

determinant for its vegetative existence; its skin and its oral zone ... are accented fields of a total experience ... "

2 I am indebted to my colleague, Dr A.B.J. Plaut, London, for this material.

3 An analogy to this capacity is given in the general processes of life by which inorganic states are changed into organic states of a higher order. Cf. to this problem Jung, CW 8, par. 375.

4 That there was a certain awareness of the psychic aspect of the *opus* is expressed in such ideas as that of the *exaltatio animae* out of its natural matrix. In one of the oldest texts we read' "Anima vero est super naturam, et per eam cognoscitur naturam". Strictly speaking, we have therefore to assume two aspects of the alchemical opus: " ... on the one hand the practical chemical work in the laboratory, on the other a psychological process, in part consciously psychic, in part unconsciously projected and seen in the various transformations of matter." Jung, CW 12, par. 380.

5 This term, originally coined by Heraclitus, is used by Jung to describe "the emergence of the unconscious opposite" CW 6, par. 709).

6 It seems that to the ancients this was common belief. To them every illness was the result of divine interference, and for this reason it could only be healed by a god or by something divine. Thus the divine healer is both the illness and the medicine (cf. C.A. Meier, *Ancient Incubation and Modern Psychotherapy*, Evanston, Ill., 1967, p. 5 ff.). More than that, the divine healer — being the illness — is ill, wounded or persecuted himself. The great centaur Chiron, fosterfather of Asklepios and of so many other heroes, is afflicted with an incurable wound (cf. Carl Kerenyi, *Asklepios*, New York, 1959, p. 79). Asklepios himself is killed through the lightning of Zeus, and Artemidor says about this event: "Nobody who has been struck by the lightning, remains unknown, and so he is worshipped as god." Another ancient author, Minucius Felix, says even: *Aesculapius ut in deum surgat fulminatur*, "Asklepios was slain by the lightning so as to become a god". (Both quotations from Meier, l.c., p. 30.) This motif of the healer who is afflicted by some suffering or killed by force is a frequent occurrence in antiquity. Herakles, for instance, who is called "the averter of evil" because he averts epidemics, suffers from morbus sacer, epilepsy; and the great hero Machaon, the father of surgery, is in the end himself mortally wounded. Kerényi, in his study on the divine healer, says of Machaon: "The best physician on earth is a hero who wounds, heals, and is fatally smitten" (Kerényi, l.c., p. 84). One is forced to the conclusion that one of the archetypal features of the healer is that he is wounded himself. In this connexion it is illuminating to consider the story of the birth of Asklepios. He is the son of Apollo and of Koronis, daughter of King Phlegyas, and who is a granddaughter to Ares. When she is already pregnant with Asklepios, Koronis is at the point of starting a love affair with another man, Ischys, the son of Elatos. When the news is brought to Apollo, his sister Artemis kills the unfaithful Koronis. Her corpse is going to be burnt, but just then Apollo saves his son out of the dead body of the mother. There could hardly be a more intense symbol of the darkest darkness out of which the divine healer will be born.

The Logos of the Unconscious

Ψυχῆς ἐστι λόγος ἑαντὸν αὔξων
Heraklitus

Already in his very first publication, his doctor-dissertation of 1902 on the "Psychology and Pathology of so-called Occult Phenomena", Jung observed that we have to postulate "a highly developed intellectual activity of the unconscious".[1] It is fascinating to see how this revolutionary idea, expressed here in a rather tentative way, has become the most powerful germinative point of his whole work,[n1] leading in its consequences up to the concept of the self.

This may be understood as arising from the fact that there is an unavoidable question bound up with the concept of an intellectual activity in the unconscious: what is the subject of such an evidently intelligent and purposive process? In pursuit of this question Jung has finally come to formulate his most creative and characteristic concepts which have in fact become the keystone of the whole edifice of analytical psychology. They are the concepts, intimately related to each other, of the objective psyche with its autonomy, continuity, and purposiveness, of the non-ego, and of the self.

This cannot be the place to pursue the gradual development of this idea, interesting and worth while as such a study would be. Only a few of the later formulations of the original idea of an unconscious intellectual activity may be mentioned.

Thus, in the introductory chapter of "The Integration of the Personality", Jung has made certain remarks regarding the existence of an "ego in the unconscious realm", of a "consciousness in the unconscious". He discusses the hypothesis of the "centre of a transcendental consciousness" which cannot possibly be the human ego.[2] At the same time, he says, it has to be recognized that this hypothetical transcendental consciousness seems to have both a continuous and a purposive existence.

These remarks link up with some others in the "Introduction to a Science of Mythology", where Jung speaks of the self as the "transcendental subject of cognition.[3] It is an interesting speculation to think of this "subject" as possessing its own "organs". In particular, if we regard it as a "subject of cognition", we may assume that such a psychic entity would have its own centre of cognition, its own unconscious centre of understanding".

A still later formulation of the same concept of the "transcendental subject of cognition" seems to lend substance to such assumption. In "On the Nature of the Psyche" Jung has put forward the idea of the unconscious as a "multiple consciousness" with its own "luminosity".[4] He says that it seems justified to think of the ego-consciousness as surrounded by a multitude of little "luminosities". This hypothesis rests on the one hand on the quasi-conscious state of unconscious contents, on the other hand on the emergence of certain images which have to be understood symbolically. These last can be found in dreams and visual phantasies of modern people as well as in the historical records.

Jung illustrates this latter point from alchemy "as one of the chief sources of symbolical representations in the past". He quotes e.g. the alchemical concept of the sparks, the "radii atque scintillae" of the "Anima Catholica", the "World Soul". Some of the alchemists even seem to have some idea of the psychic nature of these *scintillae*, of the "seeds of light in the chaos" which is the "mundi futuri seminarium" ("the seed plot of a world to come", Khunrath). One of these *scintillae* is the human mind. Similar ideas are to be found in the "lumen naturae" of Paracelsus, the "sensus naturae" which according to Agrippa of Nettesheim is characterised by "luminositas", or the "anima mundi" which is identified with the Holy Ghost.[5]

The *scintillae*, and the related concepts of the "lumen naturae" etc., correspond as "formae rerum essentiales" (Khunrath) to the archetypes. The insight of the alchemists into the nature of the *scintillae* leads to the conclusion that "the archetypes possess a certain brightness or quasi-consciousness, and that their numinositas therefore corresponds to a luminositas".

This "luminosity" would explain the existence of what we have called above the "unconscious centre of understanding". The totality of the *scintillae*, of the archetypes, produce, as it were, a "light" which becomes visible to the observing conscious mind as a consciousness in the unconscious. One *has* to postulate this consciousness in the unconscious — or, as we could also say, an "organ" of unconscious cognition — if one observes dreams and other unconscious material. Thus, when one analyses the dreams of patients — and needless to say, of "normal" people as well — one finds frequently a process of "realization" taking place in the unconscious which is so full of inner consistency, coherence, and intelligence that it possesses definitely "cognitive quality". This "cognitive" quality I have called for the purpose of this essay the "logos of the unconscious".[n2] This logos of the unconscious pursues a certain problem, as formulated perhaps e.g. in a dream, until a certain "conclusion" is reached that satisfies the particular need of the psychic moment.

I propose to illustrate this "unconscious logos", this "philosophical" process in the unconscious, by an example from a case which seems to me particularly striking in its onset, its progress, and in the "conclusion" reached. It starts with a typical "big dream" which in itself is the conclusion to a previous analytical process. In the dream a certain level of integration is reached, but at the same time a new problem begins to arise. This problem is then pursued consistently through several stages until at last a new and convincing formulation is found for the original problem, ending in a new stage of integration symbolized by the birth of the "divine child".

The dream with which I would like to start is the dream of a woman of 48 who had come for analytical treatment on account of a severe claustrophobia. The dream was dreamt about nine months after she began her treatment. Very shortly afterwards her symptoms cleared up completely and have never recurred since. In the dream she undergoes an initiation by an old woman "with a most wonderful personality". The dreamer experiences the initiation, which is "of a solemn and mystical character", in a state of ecstasy. The initiation ritual does not take place in a church, but while it proceeds the dreamer has the feeling that a kind of church — a *temenos* — is being formed round her and the initiating woman, the "hierophant".

After the initiation is over, the initiator says something about having done the same thing before with another pupil: "It happened on a train, and it is odd that the guard did not recognize us the next time, because generally they know you again; that is the only difference it makes in the outside world." After this the dreamer returns — in the dream — to her room in a hotel in order to write down what has happened, but a man in the corridor wakes her up by persistent coughing.

The significance of the initiation part of the dream is self-evident. It represents a typical *rite d'entrée* into a new community (cf. the church being formed round her) by a "wise old woman". This woman "with a most wonderful personality" would be the "priestly demonstrater"[6] of the mysteries of the "spiritual mother", of the feminine "super-ordinate personality"[7] in the woman patient. The common *temenos* being formed round the two of them would symbolize the "becoming one" with the mother goddess of the feminine initiation.

The patient herself felt that this intitiation marked a definite stage in her analysis. She felt it to be "more than a dream; it was an experience". Her claustrophobia, so she had felt, had its roots in a feeling of the meaninglessness of life and in an overwhelming fear of the world around her as a "wilderness' to which she could not relate. This fear had been something terrifyingly real and beyond rational comprehension. Analysis had made it increasingly clear that this fear of the wilderness was in fact her fear of the unconscious, due to a markedly ambivalent relationship to a very powerful and emotional mother. In other words: she had projected her fear and rejection of the "mother", of the unconscious, into the "world around her".

This fear had led her to build up an exaggerated ego-personality as a defence mechanism against the unconscious. The previous nine months of her analysis, culminating in the dream of initiation into the mysteries of the mother goddess, had on the one hand made her capable of understanding and overcoming her negative mother problem, and on the other hand had gradually revealed to her the creative side of the unconscious. Instead of being caught in a negative fixation to the personal mother, she was able to relate to the positive primordial mother.

This was summed up in the initiation dream: it appeared to her as the complete opposite and answer to the fear of the wilderness; it was real and incomprehensible like it, but whereas the experience of the wilderness was horrifying and impossible to relate to, the initiation experience was ecstatic and included her in it. She felt certain that the wilderness experience would not occur again — in other words, that she had got the better of her claustrophobia — and, in fact, it never did, since its utterly negative situation had been answered by a corresponding positive one.

Up to this point we have before us a most impressive and constructive experience of the unconscious, clear in itself and known in some form or other to all of us as one of the most convincing and satisfying experiences both to analysand and analyst. Both the content and the intensity of this symbolical experience fully explained the real change in the psychological situation of the patient as manifested in the disappearance of the neurotic symptom.

But there remain two so far unexplained episodes in the dream: the strange remark of the old woman about the guard, and the equally strange episode of the coughing man. As to the latter it seems to belong to a not uncommon type of dream in which the dreamer is woken up by some sort of interference or intervention: a telephone or an alarm clock rings, a cold wind creates a strong feeling of discomfort, a pain in some part of the body persists, or: a man coughs and wakes the dreamer up. The common denominator in each case is the "waking up" from a state of deep unconsciousness, "sleep", into a state of relatively higher consciousness. This appears either as waking up in the dream, or as actually waking up (as in our dream). In each case it refers to the need to remember a certain dream experience which would have otherwise stayed in the unconscious, and that means: lost to conscious realization.

The coughing man [n3] in our dream thus fulfils a clear function: that of forcing the transition from one level of awareness — of unconscious awareness, as it were — to another: that of conscious awareness. He has an ego-function: to connect an unconscious content with consciousness. A content of the unconscious which in itself may not yet be intense enough to reach consciousness would be a dead loss from the point of view of integration. This may, although on a different level, also explain the remark of the woman about "having done the same thing before with another pupil" but whom "the guard did not recognize next time", as if a previous initiation had taken place in the unconscious but had not reached the level of "recognition". In contrast to this previous failure of realization there has now been an adequate preparation, most likely through the progress of the analytical work. Through it the unconscious content has become intense enough to cross the threshold of consciousness, and on the other hand consciousness has become sufficiently "permeable" to the unconscious content. This corresponding progress on the part of both the unconscious content and consciousness has produced the energy needed to precipitate the symbolical realization.

The return of the woman to her room — which may be understood as a return to her previous condition — is disturbed by a masculine "interference" in the corridor, that is, "outside" her room. This interference is felt as unpleasant because it forces her out of the "sleeping" state of her still unconscious femininity. Had she not been woken up by the intervention of the masculine element, the experience of the initiation would have stayed in the unconscious. The coughing man, disturbing her "naïve" feminine existence, represents the inner urge and need for a more comprehensive personality, for higher consciousness.

What remains to be understood is the strange remark about the guard. Who is he? What does it mean to be "recognized", to be "known" by him? And what is the only "difference it makes in the outside world"?

"The guard on the train", who "guards" the movement from one place to another, is the one who "knows", who "recognizes" or refuses recognition. He knows, he has insight, he chooses and discriminates; he is the power of realization in the unconscious. In other words: he is a manifestation of the "logos" of the unconscious. This unconscious logos is aware of a change which has taken place during and through the dynamic process of initiation. His recognition seems essential: that he knows and recognizes makes all the difference, in fact the only difference in the outside world. But what is the outside world?

It could refer to the concrete, worldly, outside reality; to some reorientation, some better adjustment in actual life. Of this there is a definite sign in the disappearance of the symptom. But this would hardly need the acknowledgement of the guard; it would be sufficiently motivated and explained by the initiation as such. This in itself indicates a complete change in the patient's attitude to her unconscious. Therefore this "outside" must refer to some "outside" inside her psychic reality, in other words to something outside, beyond the meaning of the feminine initiation which has taken place: to the activation of the unconscious logos. The first step is the initiation into womanhood, but the next step is the realization that to be a woman means to be "known" by the man.

We have thus to distinguish between three distinct layers of the unconscious process. The first one is that of the initiation which has taken place, and which according to the patient's own feeling and also to the inner logic of the previous analytical process up to this point would be an adequate explanation of the clearing up of the symptom. The second layer would be that of the guard knowing, and the third layer would be that of the coughing man who has the distinct function of waking her up and thus to link the unconscious experience up with consciousness.

When the initiation seems sufficient to explain the disappearance of the claustrophobia, the fact of the guard knowing would represent a kind of surplus phenomenon. Now it is a frequently observed fact that the unconscious works with great economy of purpose. The guard is bound to be more than a sort of embellishment or afterthought. We may, therefore, assume that, if the symptom has disappeared with the initiation, the energy imprisoned in it has thus been released and become free for the next step, expressed in the figure of the guard.

This raises an interesting problem with regard to the function and significance of the neurotic symptom in our case and in other cases. We all know the type of case in which the main function of some particular symptom seems to be that it forces the patient into analytical treatment and thus into contact with the unconscious and integrative process. One cannot help feeling in such cases that the symptom is an instrument of the self where the other means have not been effective enough. The symptom then appears as a psychic stimulus through which inner events are made available to consciousness where the primary perception through other "normal" channels has been inhibited for some reason or other. (An important comment in this connection is contained in the mythologem of the "wounded healer", whose wound acts as just such an instrument of the self.)

The symptom is in this sense a manifestation of the self. This explains the apparent disproportion one feels so often between an, as it were, accidental symptom and the enormous powers released by it in the "opus magnum". It also explains the fact that the disappearance of a symptom so often seems not to be the genuine answer to the meaning and labours of the integrative process. In other words: energetically speaking, no symptom appears commensurable with the energy it releases but appears rather to be a mere trigger. When this trigger has fulfilled its function — in other words: where the symbolical meaning of the symptom has been understood — it may safely be dispensed with.

On the basis of this reasoning one would have to assume in our case that the patient's symptom has fulfilled its purpose. It has made her perceive the one and essential thing: the reality and the constructive aspect of the unconscious in her experience of the initiation. As a matter of fact from this moment onwards a clearly marked "philosphical" process, both continuous and purposive, becomes visible in the unconscious, leading up to a definite "conclusion" two months later, which to the patient seemed the final formulation of and the answer to her quest. Interesting as it would be to follow the unconscious course over these two months, we shall have to confine ourselves here to the final dreams of this process. Only this much may be said about the most characteristic dreams of this period, that they contain frequent references to a subterranean argument going on between male and female elements, with a constant stress on the importance of the first. (To give only one characteristic example: she dreamt of a certain miraculous dragonfly which cannot be properly seen except by the use of a magnifying lens through which it can and must be seen "in reflection".)

Then, just two months after the initiation dream, there emerge three dreams within a week, leading to what seems to be a satisfactory and adequate answer to the problem left open in the original dream: the knowledge of the guard and the sign by which he knows. In the first of the three the patient is with me — her analyst — and the next time she comes for analysis I am going to perform an "operation of artificial fertilization on a carp". The artificial fertilization of a fish would be a very unusual procedure. It is clearly a highly symbolical operation that is going to be performed, quite remote from the level of every-day life; so much so, in fact, as to amount to a proper "opus contra naturam" (according to the word used in the dream it would be an "operation", i.e. a human act interfering with nature). This is, by the way, the first allusion to the *opus contra naturam* in our dream material. In keeping with this the operation will be performed by the analyst in the analytical situation. The "analyst" himself carries the projection of the positive animus, of the creative logos. He can be regarded as another manifestation of the guard, but now nearer to consciousness than in the initiation dream, since he is an actual person playing a part corresponding symbolically to that attributed to him in it.

As to the carp, finally, since it is going to be fertilized, it must be a feminine fish. The feminine fish is a frequent uterus symbol, here reinforced by the particular shape of the carp. It would thus refer to unconscious femininity and receptiveness that has to be "operated" upon by masculine logos. The analyst would symbolize the creative and procreative animus in the sense that he represents the fertilizing consciousness for the still inarticulate and dim feminine spirituality (= fish).

Fertilization is the union of the female reproductive cell with the male reproductive cell, a union in which the two cells fuse into one. Symbolically speaking, our dream would thus point to a complete "coincidentia oppositorum". But fertilization also brings about a complete activation of the female reproductive cell in which it changes from an inert state into one of highest possible activity. If we regard the process of fertilization as a *coincidentia oppositorum*, then we would have to expect as a result the birth of a new attitude.

A few days after this dream — in fact the "next time she came for analysis" — she had another one which impressed her deeply. In it a man friend has been to see a famous wise man from whom he received some books and also an expanding device with which it is possible to demonstrate the Pythagoras theorem. The man friend refers to an actual friend who had met Prof. Jung and through whom she first came into contact with his psychology. He was thus responsible for her starting her analysis. In the case of both dreams — the carp dream and the last one — it is men who are the active persons, a clear sign of the activation of the creative logos side. This is reinforced by the allusion to mathematical knowledge, and, in an even higher sense, by the remote figure of the wise old man: as such he transcends the merely masculine knowledge in a higher and more comprehensive wisdom. The wise man is associated with Jung through the personality of her friend who had actually been to see him. The psychological friend is thus a mediator of the superior wisdom of the highest animus figure.

The meaning of the books is clear enough as denoting logical, scientific knowledge. But it is with the expanding device for demonstrating the Pythagoras theorem — at first sight so strange and remote — that we approach the profound meaning of the dream. The "expanding device" represents the growing power of "philosophical", spiritual, realization. But what about the Pythagoras theorem? When we discussed the dream, my patient had surprisingly no doubt or hesitation in feeling and understanding the meaning of his theorem in the context of her dream in particular and her analysis in general. To her the Pythagoras theorem carried a very definite emotional message: that when numbers are raised to a higher power, new relations are found to exist between them. According to the theorem, known to all of us, if the three sides of a triangle are a, b and c, then $a^2 + b^2 = c^2$. Yet a plus b does *not* equal c; there is no mathematical relation between them. Only when they are raised to a higher level, to a higher power, is the relation revealed, and c becomes as it were the uniting and reconciling factor.

It is most characteristic for the particular "philosophical" process in a woman that such a mathematical fact is experienced as a revelation of relationship and integration. Where a masculine attitude would have discovered mathematical and rational connections, to her the human and relational values are decisive.[n4]

The significance of the dream and its hidden "logical" message is enhanced by a dream two nights later, which the dreamer felt to be a direct continuation of and comment on the last dream. In it I, the analyst, had been speaking, and my concluding words were: ... the glory, the incredible perfection of 7^3 and 9^3."

Here an even higher power, or level, than that of the last dream seems to be indicated: whereas the first spoke of numbers in the second dimension, we are here dealing with the third. The words the analyst uses are almost ecstatic — a Pythagorean might have spoken of numbers like that, or somebody to whom the esoteric signification of numbers and mathematical operations was fully alive. One is reminded of Novalis's saying: "The true mathematician is enthusiast per se. Without enthusiasm no mathematics".[8]

The symbolism of the numbers 7 and 9 is so rich that for our purpose the barest hints must suffice. Seven is, of course, the number of initiation par excellence. It symbolizes the ascent through the 7 spheres of the planets and the 7 stages of transformation, as for instance in the mysteries of Mithras and in the alchemical process; to the Fathers of the Church "septenarius numerus est perfectionis". Jung's books, in particular his *Psychology and Alchemy*, provide such a wealth of material and illustrations that a reference to them might be sufficient.

The symbolism of the number 9 is equally widespread. First it is connected with the number 3 and is a reinforcement of the latter, which is well known as a numinous number (the number of synthesis, of the triad and the Trinity; it is the number of magic incantation etc.). But apart from its connection with the 3, the 9 has a symbolical meaning in its own right. First of all there is its obvious and highly relevant meaning connected with the months of pregnancy. Then there are the Egyptian Ennead of gods, the 9 customs, parts of the sacrifice, heavens etc. of China, the 9 worlds of the Edda etc. etc.

One could speculate a great deal on the particular significance of the 7 and 9. I shall confine myself to a few facts relevant to our material. First of all, both numbers are distinctly numinous numbers (as is, indeed, practically every simple number). The particular choice of the numbers could be understood thus: the 9 expresses the idea of the world's basic constituents,[n5] and the 7 that of their transformation. With that the 9 would have a "resting", passive, and feminine quality, and the 7 a moving, active, and masculine quality.[n6]

The combination of the two numbers would thus denote a *coniunctio*. In this connection the words "glory" and "incredible perfection" are significant: their ecstatic character would express the mystery of the *hieros gamos*, of the ecstatic moment of the union. Seven and nine would symbolize Shiva and Shakti, and from their union would spring the divine child.

Another important aspect of the dream is clearly that the two numbers are raised to the third dimension, and thus to a still higher power than that of the dream of the Pythagoras theorem. There is an ascending significance, whereas the first dream reveals the secret relation between numbers — and hence, to use the Pythagorean idea, between essential units of the universe — the second dream speaks not only of the relation between things but of their "glory" and "incredible perfection". This calls to mind the three levels of realization in Tantric philosophy: the *sthula*, the *sukshma* and the *para* aspect of things. The first, the *sthula* aspect, deals with the concrete material aspect of the world only — with its "gross" matter — and would be analogous to numbers in their first dimension. The second aspect, the *sukshma* aspect, deals with the symbolical significance of the world — with its "subtle" matter — and would be analogous to numbers in the second dimension. Finally the *para* aspect which deals with the esoteric aspect of the world — its "highest" meaning and innermost secret — would correspond to numbers in the third dimension, revealing the deepest significance and essence of the universe.

To the patient these seemingly abstract considerations had a very real and profoundly *emotional* meaning. It linked the two number dreams up directly with the great initiation dream, thus showing the inherent continuity of the unconscious philosophical process that had been going on all the time. It has been mentioned above that to the patient the meaning of the first number dream lay in the fact that on a higher level of awareness relationships are revealed which do not — or do not seem to — exist on a lower level. This was reiterated and reinforced by the second number dream in which an even higher level of realization was indicated. Her original initiation dream had given her a new relationship to the unconscious, and with it the possibility of understanding and overcoming her fear of the "wilderness" of world and life. Now, in the two number dreams, this realization is continued and moulded into a new and finally satisfying conclusion: the apparent lack of order in the universe — or psychologically speaking, in her own life and in her relationship to the world around her — was not absolutely final but was due to the limitations of her own approach and awareness. Once she could "raise" the power of her own understanding, a new and higher order became visible behind the apparent disorder.

Whereas it had been almost unbearable — witness her claustrophobia — to live in a world which seemed devoid of sense and meaning, the realization of order and relationship between things led to an almost ecstatic feeling of acceptance and relatedness. Again one is reminded of a saying of Novalis: "Pure mathematics is religion [9]." When things, when one's own understanding of things, are raised to a higher power, an order can be seen running through all of them, and also through the human mind which so far had stood helpless and confused in face of them. What is more, another conclusion is inherent in this realization: that the harmony of things, of all the components of the world, points to the existence of a uniting power which gives sense and significance to the apparently disconnected parts. The initiating woman, the guard who knows, the remote wise man who possesses the expanding instrument by which the hidden relationships can be found, the "analyst" who through the transference of archetypal images assumes a significance far transcending his person — all are manifestations of the power behind the phenomenal world. They are, as it were, messengers and tools of the self in which the conflicting and opposing parts become reconciled. Here at last, she felt, was the final answer to the "wilderness".

One more aspect of our dreams remains to be discussed, particularly of the two number dreams with their symbolical formulation of inherent significance, namely the comment they make on the remark of the initial dream: " ... that is the only difference it makes in the outside world." The dreams reopen one question inherent in this "difference", namely: on what level, under what aspect, of reality is the inner psychic event "real" and efficacious?

To analysts two kinds of analytical processes are known. The first is the one in which the symptom is cleared up, but where one feels nevertheless that the contact with the unconscious has been something peripheral and passing. These cases can perhaps be defined roughly as those in which the emphasis has been on the unconscious complexes and blockages and where their analysis achieves the desired result. Although these cases are obviously satisfactory in as much as the symptom has cleared up, there frequently remains a feeling of regret that the deeper layers of the unconscious have not been sufficiently explored and brought into play. Even when one feels quite satisfied as a psychotherapist, the "analyst" in one is regretfully aware of the limitations of the result achieved.

In contrast to this (and needless to say, there are all possible grades of transition between the two possibilities mentioned) there is the second type of case in which the full powers and potentialities of the unconscious are more or less completely activated, explored and turned to use — as shown in our material. Occasionally there even arises a puzzling paradox in so far as a really vital and constructive analytical process takes place, is acknowledged as such by the patient, and still the original symptom persists. In such cases one has to assume that the symptom serves as a constant stimulus for further assimilation.

However this may be, whether the second type of patient arrives with a definite symptom or not (for, as we all know, people often come for analysis even without any clear clinical symptom), and whether the symptom clears up or not, the crucial point is how far the integrative process of individuation arising from contact with the archetypal images will extend, and how it will develop. The answer showing the true effect and result of the *opus* evidently does not lie with the symptom, its existence or non-existence, its persistence or disappearance, but has to be sought elsewhere.

But where? This is the puzzling question which probably many of us have come across some time or other. Erich Neumann, in his 1949 Eranos lecture on "The Mythical World and the Individual", has expressed the same bewilderment when he says: "The reality and efficaciousness of such inner processes often cannot be proved, and for the 'outside' world they are as difficult to verify as the psyche itself ... It seems that the category of processes in the psychic realm is still so foreign to our consciousness that we cannot but ask for evident proof 'outside' by which this inner process could legitimize itself ... "[10]

Here the same question crops up: how the "reality" and effect of psychic processes can be "verified". For even if in our particular case the symptom has disappeared, we have to acknowledge the strange fact that often nothing tangible at all, or very little, seems to correspond to the inner feeling of transformation arising from the intimate contact with the unconscious. Where we might expect a conspicuous change of personality, a far-reaching and tangible adjustment, we may as often as not be disappointed. And yet: even in cases where nothing definable or visible has happened, there is the inner feeling of self-evidence that something constructive *has* taken place.

To this question our material seems to give a valuable and valid comment. "The only difference it makes in the outside world" — the knowledge of the guard — has, in the course of the unconscious development that started with the initiation dream, led to a realization of extreme importance. Here we seem to be able to understand the "category of the processes in the psychic realm" as the unfolding of an inner order and significance which, even where it does not become visible "outside", carries inner conviction. Its intrinsic "legitimization" does not lie so much on the plane of ordinary concrete reality as on the "higher" plane of symbolical reality above — or as we could say from another angle, "below" it — where psychic events are both factual and efficacious. They may or may not be verifiable "outside", but inside the psyche they are self-evident as a category which assigns meaning and significance, and hence establishes a most satisfactory inter-relatedness of the different psychic components on their different levels.

The birth of such a new answer to life, of a new feeling of significance, finds one of its most frequent expressions in the symbol of the birth of the inner child. Our case material confirms this symbolical pattern with a dream dreamt immediately after the climax of the two number dreams. The same night as the dream about 7^3 and 9^3, and immediately following it, the patient dreamt about giving birth to a child; for the delivery she had to go to a sage or magician. The child was a miraculous girl: perfect in shape, but smaller than an actual child. She had green eyes and on top of her head was a place which felt soft, like another eye.

This dream seems like a summing up of all that has gone before, starting with the initiation into womanhood.[n7] The initiation has, of course, to be taken in the context of the whole analytical process; no single incident in analysis can be regarded as a disconnected event. In this sense the initiation represents only a relative starting point which itself is the outcome of previous developments.

The "miraculous" characteristics of the child are evident. Her size repeats the "smaller than small and bigger than big" motif of the divine child (elf, dwarf, Tom Thumb, etc.[11]); she has snake's eyes; is delivered with the help of a magician, and has the third eye (the "pineal" eye) of spiritual vision. This divine child, the Kore, symbolizes the "superordinate personality", the self.[12] To paraphrase a well known concept in alchemy, we might call her a true "filia philosophorum". This term seems the more appropriate, as this dream child is so clearly the outcome of a "philosphical" process in the unconscious. Here the original initiation into womanhood shows its essential result: Demeter and Kore have found each other; the circle is closed with the birth of the feminine self.

The interesting thing about the birth of the self is that this "super-ordinate personality" which is being born out of the process of integration is at the same time the power which has all along been active in this very process. In other words: the self, the superordinate personality, which is the true *dynamis* behind the individuation process, gives birth to itself as it goes along. This is another formulation of the well known mythologem of the god who brings himself to birth, e.g. in the myth of the *hiranya-gharba*, the golden germ in the Prajapati hymn of the Rigveda, or in the concept of the transcendant and immanent god. The channel and tool through which the self manifests itself is the power of realization inherent in the human psyche.

Jung has pointed out how the phenomenology of the birth of the divine child "always points back to an original state of non-recognition", and how at the same time "the urge and compulsion to self-realization is a law of nature".[13] In the process of individuation this urge to self-realization — we might also say: this urge of the self to be realized — forces the individual out of his imprisonment in the state of non-recognition, of *avidya*, of darkness. The potentiality for realization is expressed in the concepts of the *scintillae* and the *lumen naturae*. They are the *anima mundi* — psychologically speaking, the self, "the world-soul [which] is a natural force, responsible for all the phenomena of life and the psyche".[14]

How in the integrative process the *anima mundi* reveals the world's "formae rerum essentiales", and in them the essential order and numinosity of life; how the self as "the transcendental subject of cognition" creates its own "cognitive" organs in the psyche, how it "thinks" its own thoughts until by the working of this "logos of the unconscious" an adequate and satisfactory answer has been found to the questions posed by our humanity — of this our material may serve as a vivid illustration.

REFERENCES

1 CW 1 par. 148.
2 Jung, *The Integration of the Personality*, (New York 1939/London 1940). pp. 15f. Cf. also CW 9.1, par. 506.
3 CW 9.1, par. 289.
4 CW 8, par. 387ff.
5 Ibid., par. 393.

6 Carl Kerenyi, in C.G. Jung and Carl Kerenyi, *Introduction to a Science of Mythology* (London, 1950; the American edition is entitled *Essays on a Science of Mythology*, New York 1949), p. 194.

7 CW 9.1, par. 309.

8 Novalis, *Fragmente* (ed. E. Kennitzer, Dresden, 1929), p. 327.

9 Ibid. Cf. also his "The life of the gods is mathematics"

10 Erich Neumann, "Die Mythische Welt und der Einzelne", in *Eranos-Jahrbuch 1949* (Zurich, 1950), pp. 233f.

11 CW 9.1, par. 267, 283

12 Ibid., par. 310, 315.

13 Ibid., par. 289f.

14 CW 8, par. 393.

NOTES

1 Michael Fordham in an article written for Jung's 70th birthday (*Brit. Journal of Med. Psychology*, Vol. XX. 3, London, 1945) has pointed out how two other ideas of great consequence have already been adumbrated in Jung's first book: the essential importance of consciousness in the therapeutic process, and the synthetic or prospective nature of the unconscious contents.

2 With this term I do not want to convey an "intellectual" quality but an intelligent, meaningful, directed, and co-ordinating faculty in the unconscious psyche. As logos of the unconscious it does neither have the "rational" quality nor the limitations of the conscious logos but expresses itself in symbolical language. It manifests itself not in a "logical" process but in a "philosophical" process, to use this term in the alchemical meaning. As "philosophical" process it would be a function of the self in the process of centroversion. Symbolically speaking, to the logos of the unconscious would be co-ordinated the moon and the stars of the night sky (= scintillae!), and not the sun of the day sky.

3 The "coughing" man is explained by an association of the dreamer: a man friend of hers had been dangerously ill in hospital. While she was talking to the doctor, she heard him coughing in the most distressing way. Later the friend told her that just in that hour he had been going through an intense experience similar to her initiation experience.

4 In other words, the logos of the unconscious, the "philosophical" process in woman, has a definite Eros quality. With regard to the basic difference between masculine and feminine spirituality cf. E. Neumann's *Amor and Psyche* (London/New York, 1956) and *Zur Psychologie des Weiblichen* (Zürich, 1953).

5 There may be some relevance in the mathematical fact that every digit of the multiple of 9 makes 9 again (e.g. 3 times 9 is 27: digit 9; 21 times 9 is 189; digit 18, digit of 18: 9). Thus it always returns to itself.

6 This seems to be confirmed by a most interesting parallel to our dream which was communicated to me by a lady who is not a patient of mine. She had the dream at the age of 38, about six months after the unsatisfactory

end of a reductive analysis with practically no dream interpretation. In the dream she heard a man's (?) voice saying "with authority" the following words: "When the red bull meets the white cow, then the 7 and the 9 will also meet and that which is too good to be true will happen for mankind.

Here 7 and 9 have quite clearly masculine and feminine connotation. They are felt to be opposites whose reconciliation would be of the greatest significance. Thus, to draw a further conclusion for the meaning of our dream, one may regard the two numbers as symbolizing a pair of opposites which find their "reconciliation" on a higher plane of reality.

7 The wider implications of the dream need not be discussed in this essay; it must serve only as a final comment on the process which has been presented. Regarding the future developments in our analysis, only this much may be said: after the birth dream the unconscious situation underwent a change. At first there seems to be a sort of hiatus, and then dreams of a different character appear. They inaugurate, as it were, a new archetypal cycle of the psychic drama, circling round the problem of the opposites of good and evil.

Ego Integration and Patterns of Coniunctio

In this short essay I am going to deal with the problem of the integration of the ego from the feminine aspect. My material is, with one exception, taken from one particular case. With its help I shall try to illustrate the unfolding of the archetypal pattern of the *coniunctio*, of the union of contrasexual opposites, as starting from and based on the archetype of incest. I shall further try to show how the individual situation actualizes this archetypal pattern, in a negative way as frustrating it or in a positive way as constellating it. Although it is only a brief sketch I hope that it will help to throw light on a particular problem.

The case is that of a woman in her early forties with agoraphobia. In her case, as in other cases of agoraphobia, I found that the symptom was due to a very early disturbance of the primal relationship to the mother, of what Neumann has called the *Urbeziehung*[1] plus an incestuous problem on the side of the father. First of all, the absence of the maternal *temenos*, of a secure relationship to the mother, has produced the menace of the open space. The actual mother has proved insufficient, and has thus constellated the negative great mother. Then the infant finds it too difficult to identify with mother and suffers from lack of primal containment. In the end the infant has not succeeded in producing a secure enough ego, and the ego is, as it were, left without its proper skin, without its own protective *temenos*. Thus, on the one hand, it is constantly threatened by flowing away into the environment symbolized by the void of the open space; and, on the other hand, as a secondary phenomenon, space constantly threatens to intrude into the confines of an unprotected and too incoherent ego. This danger of intrusion gains even more reality in connection with the incest fantasy, and the latter assumes an overpowering character where the father's unconscious incestuous fantasies exert pressure from his side.

In itself the incest fantasy of the child is an archetypal pattern.

It has its forerunner in a pre-incest situation in which the infant experiences a primal *coniunctio* in containment in and identification with the relationship of the parents. In my opinion this is, strictly speaking, a pre-ego state; and in this sense, as far as the ego's partner-role is concerned, the incest fantasy represents the basic pattern of the *coniunctio*. With its content of countersexual polarity, this positive incest, as I would like to call it, is full of integrative potentialities. For the girl it is the primal archetypal experience of the creative spirit, but naturally on an unconscious level. This experience turns, on account of the personal father's unconsciousness, into a negative incest fantasy. The latter is characterized by its menacing and hostile character to which the child stays fixated. The fear of — and repressed desire for — the masculine sex in general, and incest in particular, have been adduced as a basic element in the symptomatology of agoraphobia;[2] to me it seems only a secondary although vital feature in the situation. The first condition is the faultiness of the maternal *temenos* which — in consequence — lays the child too wide open to the invasion of unassimilable contents, to the attack by the father's unconscious fantasies.

The case in question runs true to form in that the individual mother was an immature and self-centred woman, who could not relate to the child in a natural way. She was dominated by an exceptionally gifted husband. On the conscious level, the father had an excellent relationship to the child; it was, however, as analysis showed vitiated on the unconscious level by a strong feeling problem of the father and an anima projection on to his daughter.

The first eighteen months of treatment had been dominated by infantile material relating to the image of the "bad mother". Analysis brought to the surface how abandoned and isolated the infant had felt as a result of the faulty primal relationship. Very gradually analysis had produced a compensatory effect by creating a transference relationship in which I was experienced as the containing mother on whose undemanding love and patience she could rely. I cannot here go into the stages of restoration of this maternal *temenos*, but a dream, about eighteen months after the start of analysis, will show where we had arrived at that stage.

In the dream, she leads me, the analyst, through a flight of rooms into an inner, central hidden room where she has something very important to say. The room is very beautiful, warm and quiet, with soft light. I look very much as in reality. But suddenly I plunge my arms brutally down the opening of her dress and rape her. This "I had to do".

The two relevant facts of the dream are the "inner room" and the "rape". As to the latter, the dream was a real trauma. It terrified her; she could hardly tell me of it, and she was deeply disgusted with me for my action in the dream.

But equally important was the drama which takes place in the "inner room". In this central, beautiful, soft room we have the restored and secure maternal *temenos*. It is the archetypal womb, the *krater*, inside which the feminine ego can go through a critical experience. Thus the room symbolizes the positive great mother. She can now identify with her, and in this identification the feminine ego has been established. In this sense the restored maternal *temenos* and the patient's redeemed feminine ego coincide. Now the incestuous relationship can be faced. At this point the father image, the male element, is constellated.

The negative incest fantasy, which had been activated by the faulty father-daughter relationship, has to be redeemed in the transference. The projection of the incest fantasy on to the analyst thus does not just raise the negative incest fantasy with the father into consciousness, but, just as important, it is a stepping-stone beyond it: out of the negative into the positive incest, thus anticipating the *coniunctio*.

From the inner development of the dream it is evident that the very thing she has to communicate to me is just this experience of rape. The dream is important because it shows how inside the maternal *temenos* the attack of the male can be tolerated, in fact, it is an inevitable step on the way towards individuation. The "inner room" represents the position achieved; the rape the stage continuing it. But at this point the encounter with the male is still experienced as highly ambivalent: it is both the creative and desired act, and the unexpected, traumatic assault. The male "intruder" cannot yet be fully accepted since the feminine ego is still largely identified with and contained in the great mother: the patient still wants to remain the daughter. From a different angle the ambivalence expresses the constant ambivalence of the purposes of the ego and the self: the ego is still frightened of, and may be not yet fully prepared for, the purpose of the self.

Only in parenthesis I want to add that with this dream her sexual relationship with her husband began to improve. Whereas, previously, there had been a considerable problem of sexual adjustment in an otherwise happy marriage, now, after one and a half years, the physical relationship became a source of enjoyment and pleasure.

To return to the dream, it seems that before the male intruder can be more fully accepted, a further step in ego integration has to be achieved. This step appears to be de-identification from the great mother. It is indicated in a further dream, about six months after the rape dream. In the dream, she is a little girl watching other children play in a field. Suddenly a boar rushes into the field; she is terrified, but there is a house where she knows she can take refuge. In front of the house an old woman is standing quietly; without words the woman knows all about her, and she feels safe.

First of all, the dreamer experiences herself as a child. I should like to come back to this point later on. Then there is the threatening boar, the elemental, destructive, phallic power of the great mother. On the archetypal level this destructive power is symbolized in the killing of Attis or the Zeus of Crete; on the personal level it manifests itself as the negative animus. But at the point of crisis the other pole to this destructive aspect of the great mother is constellated; the guardian and goddess of the house, of the protective maternal *temenos*, appears. There is, however, a very different side to the ambivalent situation. John Layard, to whom I am much indebted in this respect, has drawn my attention to the positive significance of the boar, confrontation with whom is, as he put it in a written communication, "one of the great transforming situations of archetypal significance". To put it very briefly, the boar is also the archetypal male and the encounter with it represents the confrontation with positive incest.

On one level the old woman is the manifestation of the positive great mother who protects her, but on another level she would be the devouring mother who holds on to the child, and, by drawing her from the open field into the house, would prevent her encounter with the male. The dream then shows a great uncertainty and hesitation on the part of the feminine ego: at this point either she may still be unable to cope with the boar and, therefore, be in real need of the protection of the great mother; or she may simply cling to her protection in order to avoid the next step — that is, confrontation with the creative great father in the act of positive incest.

In spite of the manifest fear and hesitation, the dream takes the pattern of the *coniunctio* a stage beyond the rape-dream. For one thing, in the boar-dream the ambivalence, and with that the reality, of both female and male archetypal powers, are fully realized; for another, the female encounter with the male, though not yet consummated, is no longer bound up with the person of the analyst. True, it is still an incestuous situation in that the dreamer experiences herself as child; but, on the other hand, the male is, in the figure of the boar, experienced as elemental archetypal power.

The ambivalence of the dream indicates an unfinished situation, and points towards an encounter with the male as transpersonal power; an encounter yet to be accepted. The fact that the dream-ego appears as a child expresses a basic ambivalence: on the one hand, the ego is bound to feel inferior to the archetypal force of the non-ego; but, on the other hand, there is also the indication that the child can no longer depend on maternal protection in her encounter with the male. In this sense the sexual experience with the analyst in the rape-dream had been a rehearsal for the next stage of the *coniunctio* in which the frightened but established ego has to step out into the open. Now it has to maintain itself in its independence; identification with and containment in the great mother have to be sacrificed.

I want to point out only in parenthesis the significance of the enclosed space in the first dream and of the open field in the second with regard to the problem of agoraphobia: here again the encounter on the open field represents an important step beyond the protection of the inner room.

A remark which the patient made a short time after the last dream was characteristic of the inner development initiated with it. She expressed her feeling that a new stage in analysis had been reached. She described it by saying: "My interest in mother seems exhausted, and I know that now 'sex' is the important thing." With "sex" she meant to convey something much wider than the physical experience; as it were, "Sex" with a capital S, symbolizing the encounter with "Father" — again with a capital F — and with the male in general.

How real this new stage of realization and ego-integration was showed itself when, several months after the boar-dream, the patient was able to go out on her own for the first time since the start of the analysis. She had learned to face and accept the male without running back into her mother's arms.

A new phase and a new pattern of the *coniunctio* manifest themselves in another dream about eight months after the boar-dream. In the dream she is lying in bed, nobody else is in the room, but then quite unexpectedly, something incredibly strong, like an electric current or a whirlwind, completely penetrates and seizes her whole being, rapes her, but without any negative connotation of the word: it is like an invasion by something superhuman, to which resistance would be both impossible and senseless. In the dream she said the words: "Now it can happen."[n1] The experience was so strong that she shook uncontrollably.

Here again we have an experience of rape, of invasion. The patient herself connected it with the first rape-dream. She felt the last dream to continue and complete the first one in two respects. First, whereas the earlier dream had been traumatic, there was no feeling of trauma or any idea of resistance in the latter; in spite of its overpowering character it seemed wholly acceptable. Secondly, whereas the rape-dream was still bound to the person of the analyst, the current was impersonal and numinous in quite a new way. She felt the whole experience to be deeply creative. Perhaps we can say that at this point the boar of the previous dream had penetrated her with his tusk-phallas, no longer killing but fertilizing; the ambivalence of the destructive-constructive great father has been synthesized in the fusing current of the transpersonal male.

Both the creative experience and the inherent limitation of this stage are self-evident. On the one hand, in the encounter with the numinous invader, the patient can completely submit to the masculine partner, and in her feminine surrender she becomes transformed. On the other hand, she is as yet only a passive recipient for the power of an impersonal and completely dominant male opposite. Further development of the pattern of the *coniunctio* will have to go in the direction of gradual equalization of the two partners and a growing individualization of the relationship. I should like to illustrate two further stages by two dreams.

The first one occurred about ten months after that of the invading current. In the dream a man who had always been to the patient the embodiment of positive spirit, but of whom for this very reason she had been rather frightened and full of inferiority feelings, talks to her in a tender understanding way of her "Beauty". Again, like "Sex" in the previous dream, "Beauty" meant much more than the word as such conveys: it was the essence of femininity, and she felt deeply appreciated and recognized.

This dream shows an individualized relationship. It is also one of relative equality, although the initiative and preponderance of the man are still clearly marked. He is a kind of liberator who helps the woman to realize and accept her feminine individuality. With that a mature relationship is ushered in; the two partners become more and more equals, and a meeting of two individuals can take place. This is meant to include both external and internal relatedness: on the actual plane of outer reality two integrated individuals can meet in creative exchange, and on the symbolical plane of inner reality woman can experience man as an inner creative partner. This represents the final stage of the *coniunctio* which leads to the birth of the divine child, the self. On account of the mutuality of relationship the experience of man is on this level, *mutatis mutandis*, identical with that of woman.

For both its clinical and theoretical importance I would like to mention here the close correspondence of the development sketched out by the dreams with that given by Neumann in his research on feminine psychology. He starts off with the primal relationship, the *Urbeziehung*, in which the infant is contained inside the "maternal *uroboros*" [3]. He calls this phase that of "self-preservation" which is ended by the invasion of the "patriarchal *uroboros*".[4] In my material we have first the containment in the inner room of the maternal *uroboros*; this phase of self-preservation is challenged in the ambivalence of the boar-dream. It is finally ended with the invasion by the impersonal numinous current. As next stage Neumann describes that of the patriarchate[5], which is expressed in my patient's material in the dream of the man making her aware of her feminine "Beauty". After this, according to Neumann, there follow two further stages; that of the "meeting", *Begegnung*, between two individuals, and that of "individuation", of inner realization.[6] I prefer actually to see his two consecutive stages as the two aspects, outer and inner, of one and the same pattern of the *coniunctio*.

I would like to illustrate this final stage by a last dream, this time of another woman patient, aged fifty-three, who, in an analysis lasting over five years, had gone through an intense process of integration. This is the dream:

> I have just been married; my husband is a prince, wise, gentle, and loving. He puts a gold ring with an engraved flower on the third finger of my left hand. Then we are searching for ingots of gold which have been buried in a field. It is the royal treasure which has been hidden during times of trouble. We search a square patch of ground; at the edges we find nothing, but in the middle are the ingots of shining gold.

There is no longer invasion or inequality, but a loving relationship concluded under the sign of the "golden flower". It is consummated in the common search for the gold which had been hidden during the troubled times of neurosis. The treasure is found in the centre of the square *temenos*, varying the symbolism of the "jewel in the lotus".[7]

To conclude, I want to sum up my material in terms of comparative patterns of the *coniunctio*, i.e. of the relationship between ego and non-ego. I began by describing the negative incest relationship which is in itself neurotic. In it a rudimentary ego is confronted with an overwhelming non-ego in projection on to a negative father. It is redeemed in the positive incest relationship in which a small but intact ego is confronted with a large non-ego in projection on to a positive father. In our case the negative incest situation had to be resolved through the transference on to the analyst. In the rape-dream the ego, which by now has become more stable and coherent, experiences the ambivalence of the non-ego in projection on the father-analyst. This dream marks the transition from the negative to the positive incest-fantasy. In the boar-dream the containment in the maternal *temenos* is realized in its relativity, and the ego faces the ambivalence of both female and male archetypal powers.

After that, in the experience of the current, an ego which is now intact can be confronted with the creative non-ego, at this point no longer in projection but as inner spiritual power. Here the incestuous claim on to the father-analyst is sacrificed and transformed, and we have reached the stage of what I would like to call the "internalized transference". At first, in the invasion by the "patriarchal *uroboros*", the ego is still only the passive, recipient vessel to the power of the anonymous non-ego; but with the next stage of the "patriarchate" a progressive approximation between ego and non-ego sets in. The *coniunctio* reaches its final pattern in the stage of individualized relationship and individuation. Here female and male, ego and non-ego, meet as equal partners of creative relationship.

REFERENCES

1 Erich Neumann, *The Child* (tr. R. Manheim, New York, 1973), chapter 1 and his *Zur Psychologie des Weiblichen*, Zürich, 1953.

2 Otto Fenichel, *The Psychoanalytic Theory of Neurosis*, (New York/London, 1945) pp.196, 208.

3 Neumann, *The Child*, p.10 and passim; *Zur Psychologie des Weiblichen*, p.4.

4 Neumann, *The Child*, pp.96ff; *Zur Psychologie des Weiblichen*, pp.10-15.

5 Neumann, *The Child*, Chapter 4.

6 Neumann, *Zur Psychologie des Weiblichen*, p.51.

7 CW 12, par. 133; note 11 to par. 139.

NOTES

1 Cf. the analogous experience described in my *The Living Symbol* (London/ New York, 1961), Chapter IX, "The Fight with the Angel".

On the Question of
Meaning
in Psychotherapy

If I undertake to talk about the question of meaning in psychotherapy, it has to be understood from the outset that we are
dealing here with a most personal matter. It is highly personal
concern for a patient entering an analysis as well as for the
analyst who has to try to find his personal answer. In this sense I
hope my words will not be understood as an attempt to lay down
general rules but rather as my own confession which has its roots
in forty years of work with people suffering from one problem or
the other.

I also would like to add something which may appear self-
evident, namely that the intimate analytical situation between
two people always takes place against the background of the
collective situation. In other words, the psychic situation of the
individual, in spite of its uniqueness, is still deeply connected with
the particular problems and meaning of our time. Patient and
analyst are always confronted with this twofold question: the
question of the meaning of our subjective inner personal life and
the question of the meaning of the collective social life. These two
aspects of meaning are intimately interconnected. On the one
hand, the collective-social problems are bound to exert their
influence on us and, on the other hand, we are always challenged
to make our contribution, however small, to the collective-social
situation around us.

Anything that is played out by and in the individual, who is at
once the subject and object of psychological experience, is
inalienably connected with the collective events around him, and
individual problems are ultimately the expression of the more
general history of man. And what age could be more uncertain
and more in need of healing than ours? We must, to be sure,
guard against the fatal and almost unavoidable error of every

age, which regards itself as the only time that has ever been — and yet as the end of time. We know only too well how every age has a tendency to look back upon some earlier period as the Golden Age and, in strange contradiction, to regard its own achievements and attitudes as the finally valid ones. Yet, keeping in mind this eternal source of human error, there are nevertheless two facts that are characteristic of our time. The first, which we share with all great times of crisis, is the extensive loss of binding, organic associations, and hence of creative rituals that, by their very numinosity, would naturally bring us into contact with archetypal processes.

Here I am leaving out of account the relatively small number of people for whom collective religious ties are still valid. For the great majority the hypertrophy of ego-consciousness and rationality has led to increasing inner rootlessness and isolation. This isolation has, in its turn, found a highly problematical answer for itself in new mass movements, in which the individual gives up the most precious and the most dangerous acquisition of humanity — consciousness of himself as an individual — for the sake of a false sense of oneness and security. Characteristically, the hypertrophy of ego-consciousness goes hand in hand with a loss of genuine individuality, which is always rooted in a suprapersonal background.

The other fact — and this does indeed seem to be something completely new and unique — is that for the first time in history mankind had been given the means to decide its own continuance or destruction. This causes a profound uncertainty and anxiety all over the globe, but at the same time it challenges man to an intensive reorientation and a new responsibility. It is, after all, one and the same consciousness that is capable of leading him to knowledge of himself and of the powers around him, and simultaneously puts in his hands the means to annihilate himself and thus annul Creation at one stroke — a truly fateful and numinous decision! Today we know only too well how an isolated consciousness can lead to the most tragic blunders and false decisions when cut off from the matrix of the timeless unconscious.

It is an instructive coincidence that Freud's earliest writings, which for the first time gave the unconscious a central place in psychology, appeared at a period of general unrest and unease in European culture. We are here confronted with a real problem of a "turn of the century", and its repercussions have lasted down to our own day. This cultural unrest may be a sign either of decadence or of renewal and, as so often, it manifests itself also in art. The genuine artist is intuitively ahead of his time and is the first to sense its problems. Jung has pointed out that "art represents a process of self-regulation in the life of nations and epochs,"[1] and so "is best fitted to compensate the inadequacy of the present."[2] In this sense Worringer says in his *Abstraction and Empathy*, now become a classic, that a psychology of the need for art, of the need for style, would be "a history of the feeling about the world and as such, would stand alongside the history of religion as its equal."[3]

Of great relevance to our theme is Worringer's well-known formulation concerning the "need for empathy" and the "urge to abstraction." For him, the "need for empathy" is expressed in the style that is associated with "the sensation of happiness that is released in us by the reproduction of organically beautiful vitality".[4] In contrast to this, the "urge to abstraction" is the consequence and expression of a "great inner unrest inspired in man by the phenomena of the outside world",[5] or as we could say, slightly expanding the formula, a loss of certainty in regard to man's place in the cosmos. The urge to abstraction expresses an instinctive longing for forms that conform to law "in which man can rest in the face of the vast confusion of the world picture".[6]

If we apply these formulations to the question of the meaning of our time, we find ourselves directly confronted with the phenomenon of a fundamental anxiety, expressed in art as the artist's uncertainty in relation to his visible material and, more generally, in a growing tension between man and world, individual and reality, inside and outside. In other words, man is beset by doubts about the meaning of life, chaos threatens, and the ten thousand things have revealed their questionable character. The problem of the relationship of subject and object has been posed and where a constructive answer is attempted, as in art, more and more it is sought and found within, in man's relationship to the inner object, to the "thing in itself", which has to be abstracted and distilled from the chaotic multiplicity of the external world.

This struggle for an inner point of vantage, for knowledge of an inner reality in which the fragmentation of the outer reality can find synthesis and a new meaning, comes to expression in some of the leading artists of this century. Thus Paul Klee, in his diary, wrote of the need for an "orientation towards the Beyond". [7] Such an orientation, which leads "beyond" the conflict between man and world, subject and object, is an orientation *inward*, a turning toward the psychic center and universal ground of all reality. Another pioneer of modern art, Kandinsky, expressed this as the "Greater Reality",[8] and Franz Marc spoke of his "yearning for indivisible being", for "liberation from the sensory illusions of our ephemeral life",[9] of his search for the "inner mystical construction",[10] and said that his aim was to "disclose an unearthly being that dwells behind all things".[11]

What do these formulations of Klee, Kandinsky, and Marc express if not the artist's reaction to the increasing externalization and materialism of the twentieth century, his affinity with the prophetic knowledge of the eternally valid, archetypal world of the psyche — the "Greater Reality" of the "inner mystical construction"? Thus the increasing disappearance of the external object in the painting of the last three generations, the artist's growing concern with fantasy, association, dream images, and symbols, is an attempt to take the inner world as seriously as the outer world of objects, and to give it equal if not greater importance.

That there is a parallel development in poetry and music, and in all the arts, goes without saying. Wherever creative energies are at work, we can see how man's feelings, instead of being naively turned outward, are becoming oriented to the inner centre. Tragic and painful as this alienation from the world may be, it is also constructive and full of promise for the future. It throws up new questions which compel new answers, and the enforced recognition that life and the world are not a pre-established harmony, and that the individual's position in the cosmos faces him with problems, gives a dynamic impulse to the urge for self-knowledge.

Thus, when we view the crisis of the individual in a broader setting, it seems as if, beneath all the desolation of his existence, a deeper and eternally indestructible unconscious, a kind of universal Self, was seeking the answer to his conflicts. For, at bottom, the feeling of crisis and catastrophe is in itself a secondary phenomenon, a reaction to an empty pseudo-certainty and sterile systematization. Uncertainty and desperation are more vital reactions than smug complacency and a sterile belief in progress. The feeling of dereliction that is at last penetrating into man's consciousness is fundamentally a numinous occurrence — herein lies the justification of existentialism as a provisional attempt at reorientation — since its very emptiness forces man to confront the world and the question of his existence in it. The problem of the meaning of life thus becomes acute.

We can now see how such a question owes its existence to a situation of crisis. It shows that "meaning" is no longer self-evident and taken for granted, that our life is no longer rooted in a background of *a priori* meanings, and that meaning itself has become questionable and "doubt-full". In other words, the question of meaning arises for us only after we have been expelled from the paradise of instinctive, preconscious, immediate certainties; it presupposes expulsion from a state of containment and *participation mystique* where meaning has not yet begun to be questioned. Wherever we encounter this question or whenever we ourselves are compelled to ask it, a painful birth has already taken place — an expulsion from the womb of unquestioned containment in a collective context of meanings that are often totally unconscious. The question of meaning presupposes the loss of meaning, the experience of meaninglessness, of chaos.

In this connection we need only remember Jung's experience with the Pueblo Indians,[11] whose daily rite of helping their father, the sun, in his journey across the sky gave them their special and meaningful place in the world. It is just this consciousness that our lives have a cosmic function and suprapersonal meaning that we have lost. Jung has often pointed out that many people in a crisis can no longer find their way back to a religious collective and end up in a vacuum. Looking around for help in their predicament, they find no answer to the meaning of their lives, or of life in general, in a living, organic ritual, but feel themselves isolated and lost.

It is at this point that modern depth psychology and psychotherapy have their place and function. In their concentration on inner images and events, and their insistence on the necessity of inner experience, they are symptoms of our time, and attempts to answer the crucial questions. By far the most urgent of these is the question of the meaning of individual life and of life in general.

Psychotherapy is not in itself a new phenomenon. It is as old as mankind, and it ranges from the primitive ritual of the medicine man to religious systems and modern convulsion therapy and chemotherapy. But depth psychology and its use as a method of healing, called analysis for short, occupies a special position in this hierarchy. It is characterized by three things: first, its deliberate concentration on what is very inadequately described as "the unconscious" and the importance it attributes to this; second, the attempt to modify an unadapted attitude of consciousness by progressive integration of unconscious contents; and lastly, the unique and specific relationship between analyst and patient as expressed in the transference and countertransference. Analysis has come to be very much more than an instrument of ordinary therapy understood as the cure of a symptom. Analysis as we understand it has revolutionized the whole picture of man and, extending far beyond the walls of the consulting room, has put the understanding of his motives and actions on a new basis. The lowest and highest motives, the most destructive as well as the most creative acts, have been subjected to new and revolutionary interpretations, and made accessible to new insights.

For the sake of accuracy I must mention, though it will be obvious to all my readers, that I am using the terms psychotherapy and analysis in the particular sense that they have inside the framework of analytical psychology. However pioneering Freud's insights were, and however revolutionary in regard to the special problems of the false civilization of "progress" at the end of the last century, they ignored — partly intentionally and partly unintentionally — the great archetypal question of meaning. Classical psychoanalysis would not consider it a fit subject for analytical treatment, or, more probably, would regard it wherever it occurs as a resistance on the part of the patient behind which his "real" (i.e., infantile-sexual) problems are carefully concealed. Deeply as Freud's genius probed beneath the surface of his age, he was still so much influenced by its rationalistic trends that he could understand instinct only as a biological phenomenon that left no room for such "unscientific" problems as the question of meaning. This is where Jung's analytical psychology comes in: even though it is directed toward the sickness of the individual, it goes beyond the bounds of a pure therapy of the neuroses and expands into a cultural psychology, in which "sickness" is a symbol and starting point for wider insights. In such a context the question of meaning assumes a special importance.

For where are these problems of loss of meaning, of threatening chaos, of isolation and uprootedness, more acute than in the neurosis of the individual, and where is the compelling need for new insights and new adaptation greater and more inescapable? Where is the question of meaning more starkly presented to us than in the individual who suffers from his own meaninglessness, which perhaps first forces itself upon him as the so-called "meaninglessness" of his neurotic symptom?

Even though the meaning of the suffering, and hence of the sufferer's life, may make an immediate impression on the psychotherapist, it should not be thought that the majority of our patients come to us with questions of this kind. On the contrary, most of them come with quite concrete neurotic symptoms which — meaning or no meaning — they want to get rid of as quickly as possible. And who can blame them? For them the most obvious and impressive thing about the symptom is that it hinders them in all their normal endeavors and aspirations. Success in their profession or their value as sexual partners is jeopardized; they sleep badly or have irrational fears, and so on. For most patients their neurosis is of the same order as measles or constipation. A process of inner education initiated by the analysis itself is needed to enable them to look behind the scenes, and to see through the foreground aspect of the symptom to the deeper suffering that lies hidden behind. Only then is it possible to accept the symptom as a highly personal possession and personal problem. But once this has happened, the analysis has led to a decisive step: the patient has, in effect, declared himself ready to take himself seriously and to submit his problem to the most accurate scrutiny. By taking himself seriously he has accepted himself in his human uniqueness as a suffering individual. Whereas, before, he identified with the collective values all around him (success, self-esteem, and so on) and with the sham truths of the "normal" man, he is now faced with his own highly individual psychic crisis.

The "foreground aspect" of the neurotic symptom is confined to the disagreeable inconveniences it brings with it. Behind these lies the essential and constructive aspect of the symptom as a function of the total psychic process. From this point of view, the symptom appears both as a warning and as an indirect help arising out of the depths of the unconscious psyche, calling the individual back to himself and opening the way into the unconscious.

This is where the truly incomprehensible and irrational part of the analytical process begins: the rational normal person — normal except for the "negligible" drawback of a neurotic symptom — not only has to acknowledge the non-rationality of what now confronts him in the unconscious; he also, to a very large extent, has to be willing to deliver himself up to it. We must realize that we are here expecting of the so-called normal person something that requires great courage and a moral decision of an entirely new kind that he recognize and accept himself as "abnormal" and directed by non-rational factors. We, who are familiar with such connections from our daily experience, know that the question of life's meaning is often at the bottom of a patient's impotence, claustrophobia, or depression. But can we quite appreciate what a dangerous step into the non-rational we are demanding of our patients when we expect them to submit to the guidance of the unconscious?

Hitherto we have considered the symptom from the standpoint of the patient. But for us psychotherapists, too, its meaning and function pose entirely new questions. Basically, the question of its meaning contains in a nutshell the further question of the meaning or meaninglessness of the psychic process and of psychic life in general. This is seen most clearly from the enigmatic role which the symptom often plays in practical analysis. Let me now say a few words about the neurotic symptom and how it appears to the psychotherapist.

It very often happens that patients come with neurotic symptoms that can be cured fairly easily and quickly. They naturally give up analysis as soon as possible afterward, but the analyst often has the feeling that they have been cheated of the vital meaning of their neurosis, and that the symptom was only the beginning of a process of individuation. Conversely, there are those puzzling cases where an individuation process is clearly going forward, with a genuine expansion of consciousness and a deepening of the personality, and yet the symptom remains apparently unassailable. What happens in these cases is difficult to define. It may be that for such people the symptom acts — and must act — as a constant source of impulses, lacking which the newly won level of consciousness would get lost again. Or perhaps we have here the same archetypal constellation as is expressed in the myth of Chiron, the father of surgery, whose never-healing wound symbolizes the eternal nature of the riddle of life which can never quite be solved.[n1]

So in the curability or incurability of a neurotic symptom we have another largely non-rational factor. The only answer we can hazard is the conjecture that the self directs the dynamic process engendered by the symptom, just as it directs the process of healing which develops when the dynamics of integration are so firmly meshed with the centre of personality that the severe suffering caused by the symptom can be dispensed with. The severe suffering caused by the symptom, but not all suffering whatever: for suffering, uncertainty, and disorientation are part of every individuation process and probably also of every creative process. The converse is also true, that suffering and loss of certainty often make possible the first step along the way of individuation, or forcibly bring it about.

This paradoxical situation, in which the symptom persists although the patient has had the evident experience of a decisive and positive development and a genuine transformation, confronts us with a new aspect of the question of its meaning. What are the criteria for meaning or unmeaning in such a situation? Is someone really "cured" if the analysis has caused his symptom to disappear without having forced him to gaze into the depths of his unconscious, and how are we to understand "healing" in the case of a patient whose genuine confrontation with those depths has nevertheless not led to a cure of the symptom? In the former case we cannot be certain that an essential contact has not taken place subliminally; in the latter case perhaps we simply lack the necessary new criteria. In his comments at the end of Professor Hauer's Tantra Yoga seminar in 1932, Jung pointed out that the *para* aspect of Hindu philosophy was for us a purely theoretical abstraction,[12] just as the highest *chakras* of Kundalini Yoga transcend our concrete understanding and would be explicable only in a distant future. On this analogy we might say that for us, with our relatively primitive level of consciousness, certain processes of psychic change cannot be consciously experienced and are indefinable, although they demonstrate their reality by the evidence of their effects, and perhaps will be explained only when our consciousness has reached a higher level of development. Furthermore, processes that from the standpoint of the rational ego seem full of meaning may be quite meaningless when seen from the standpoint of the self, and conversely, the ego often has no understanding of processes that, for the self, are meaningful and creative.

So it may be that the continuance of a symptom is the precondition for subliminal experiences of meaning — a paradox which our consciousness finds hard to understand only because it is bound to concrete realities. But the sufferings of the artist and the creative processes that are often associated with illness might give an inkling of these connections. They were expressed very convincingly by a patient of mine. She suffered from a phobia, and though it had been eased by a long and thoroughgoing analysis it had by no means disappeared. Nevertheless, she had the distinct feeling that the analysis had brought about a central change and a new orientation. Once when we were discussing this paradox of a decisive development on one side and the continuance of the symptom on the other, she said: 'My phobia has opened me up and made me very receptive. When you are delivered up to fear, you are delivered up to other things as well." In these words she expressed what one might venture to call the numinosity of the symptom: it was precisely through the experience of being delivered up to fear that she became aware of forces that far transcend the ego, and could open herself to them. "What a price!" the ego may retort. But the profound connection between suffering and being opened up to these forces is an enigma that far exceeds the ego's powers of understanding.

How little we still know of these subliminal connections was once proved to me by a sad and yet again joyful experience. A few years after the successful conclusion of a deep analysis, a patient of mine, a woman in her early fifties, suffered a number of strokes which left her in a helpless and apparently imbecilic condition. It was pitiful to see a highly intelligent and cultivated human being falling back into a primitive and almost bestial state. I visited her regularly, but the human contact that had survived at first became each time more fragmentary. She then had a final attack, after which the doctors gave her up for good. I visited her one more time, feeling that a merciful release might at last be granted to such an empty life. I sat by her bed holding her hand, which seemed incapable of any kind of response. Suddenly and completely unexpectedly, she lifted herself up, turned her face toward me, and in a clear voice said: "I have seen the star over the mountains." These were her last words to me; soon afterwards she died. To this very day I am filled with thanks that I was permitted to hear these words; for they made it quite clear to me that beneath this horrific state of degeneration a process was going on which was inaccessible to all of us, and perhaps most of all to the patient herself. Little as we can say about such a process, it was evident that in spite of all the physical and mental decay, the psyche had still preserved its integrity. However deep down beneath her consciousness its life flowed, it still remained vital and creative enough to communicate at the last with a friend, and perhaps also with itself.

How infinitely close together here are meaning and unmeaning! And to what new insights may we yet attain in the future once we have learned to understand a little better the deepest layers of the psyche! Even if, strictly speaking, our last example is outside the range of analysis, it can still make a direct contribution to a better understanding of the analytical process and the role of the symptom. For it is at least possible that in this patient the individuation process, which had begun in analysis and had led to a satisfying answer, was still going on in those unfathomable depths. If I cautiously try to formulate what may have happened, I should say that the illness which cut her off more and more from the outside world had opened a door into the inner world — "a window into eternity".[13] This is what I mean by the numinosity of the symptom.

However that may be, the meaning of the symptom as a "last resort" of the total psyche, by means of which it protests against the violation of its true nature, is one of the most impressive and most constant experiences for us as psychotherapists, and one of the most momentous. It demonstrates to us the structure of the psyche as a self-regulating system, and also the dynamics of centroversion, which strives for meaning and wholeness. How these dynamics work out in a positive sense I shall now try to discuss.

* * *

Whereas at first, I tried to approach the question of meaning from its negative side, starting with loss of meaning and the problem of the neurotic symptom, and endeavoured to make the symbolic significance of the symptom clear, I would like now to attempt to find a positive answer, to formulate what the experience of meaning is as a positive reality and how it manifests itself during an analysis.

What I have to say must, in accordance with our theme, be confined to the question of meaning in psychotherapy. This is indeed a limitation, for quite obviously the experience of meaning as such is not restricted to the analytical situation. Nature, religion, art, human relationships — all these things can, because of their archetypal reality, lead to a spontaneous experience of meaning. Let me give you but one example to illustrate the spontaneity of this experience. It made a powerful impression on me, and has always remained in my mind as evidence that the spontaneous revelation of meaning is a gift of grace. It happened to a boy of fifteen or sixteen. As we know, certain critical periods of development — birth, puberty, the climacteric, and death — are like nodes of archetypal experience, and at these times the concentrated force of the suprapersonal images can easily break through the boundaries of the ego, whether in a positive or a negative sense. It was in just such a situation, when he was open and receptive to the exhilarating crisis of puberty, that illumination was granted to this boy. One day, as he bit into a particularly beautiful and delicious apple — we might call it the ideal apple, the "apple *an sich*" — there suddenly shot through him a profound and incontrovertible knowledge of the harmony of the world. An utterly convincing and rapturous experience of the indestructible order and meaning of the cosmos flooded through him and, as he related when he was a grown man, never afterward left him. Even in critical and dangerous situations it was still alive somewhere in the background. Here, very evidently, was an experience of the "eating of the world," of which the Taittiriya Upanishad speaks:[14] the ecstatic union with the cosmic order, the oneness of the ego with the apple that symbolized the beauty of the world, was experienced in an ego-transcending act of grace, in an inrush of the numinous.[n2]

That such an invasion of the unconscious can also inundate the ego in a negative sense we know from Jung's example of the lovesick young man whose cosmic experience of the starry heavens abruptly landed him in the asylum.[15]

Spontaneous experiences of meaning like the "eating of the world" are relatively rare, if we disregard initiation experiences of a different structure such as occur in religious ritual. For most people the question of meaning becomes the starting point for a long and hazardous night sea journey. That is why at the beginning of an analysis we often find dreams of journeys and of dangerous expeditions, and the fight with the dragon is the preliminary trial that has to be met before the goal is reached. But this constellation does not belong to my present theme. Rather, I shall turn back to the problem of what we mean by "meaning", and how it is experienced in analysis.

At the beginning of this essay I pointed out that the problem of meaning grows out of the experience of meaninglessness, of loss of meaning. In contrast to the *a priori* meanings postulated by religion, and also to the spontaneous experience of meaning, analysis is as a rule concerned with a situation of crisis. When we spoke of meaning and loss of meaning we were using this word as though we knew what it meant. But now, it seems to me, we must try to define more closely the content of this fundamental concept. For although we have an instinctive feeling about what we describe or experience as meaningful, it is very difficult to give a definition of meaning and loss of meaning. We might say that something appears meaningful to us when it seems "right" or "to fit."

But here we are still moving in the realm of tautologies, for when we feel something to be "right" we already feel it to be "meaningful." We have merely equated "right" and "fitting" with "meaningful" and can use the terms interchangeably without being any clearer about their content. Jung once remarked that the teleological aspect of "fitness" in biology would have to be formulated in psychology as *meaning*;[16] in other words, the experience of meaning amounts to an experience of psychic fitness, or a sense of purpose. But even the word "fitness" is rather indefinite and demands empirical clarification. I shall therefore attempt to get at the empirical content of "meaning" and the experience of it with the help of two dreams. Both dreams come from the same dreamer, a woman in the second half of life, and were dreamt at an interval of about eight weeks. They are short and full of meaning, and for this reason they seem to me eminently suited to our purpose. This is the first dream: *I am making a ground plan, perhaps of a house and garden, in which several pieces have to be fitted into a given space. They will go in quite well, only first it is necessary to draw the circle showing the points of the compass, to give the orientation. I look for something with which to draw the circle.*[17]

I will briefly sketch the interpretation of the dream as it resulted from analytical work. Both the patient and I took the ground plan as the basic plan of the empirical personality. This interpretation was supported by the fact that several "pieces" had to be fitted into a given space: the different aspects and — at present — isolated parts of the total personality, its "part souls", must find their right place in it in order to realize the plan of totality. The total personality is symbolized by the house or garden, a *temenos* with special emphasis on the feminine element. Here I need only mention the house as symbol of the Great Mother, and the garden or *hortus conclusus* as symbol of the Virgin Mary. In an extended sense the garden would also be the "philosophical" garden, a symbol of individuation.

Of great importance is the dream statement that in order to complete the task a circle has first to be drawn. It must be quartered by lines showing the four points of the compass, thus giving clear orientation and at the same time determining the centre. This circle, like the *temenos*, is a mandala symbol, and the question arises as to the relationship of the *temenos* (house or garden) to the circle divided into four. The dreamer felt it as important that it was not the ground plan itself which was represented as a circle divided into four. The division into quarters, she felt, made the circle an image of "cosmic orientation". Here we need only remember Jung's definition of the mandala as a "psychic center of the personality not to be identified with the ego."[18] Whereas the ground plan would represent the scope of the empirical personality, the circle divided into four signifies a higher plane of orientation. The dreamer felt that this higher orientation was necessary before the ground plan could be properly constructed. Only against the background of the transpersonal self does the empirical personality fall into place and find its meaning.

Another important association of the dreamer was that in some indefinable way, which was nevertheless quite clear to her, the circle and the ground plan were identical. This expresses the fact that the empirical personality, in which all the "part souls" are organically fitted together as a personal self, would, like the suprapersonal self, be symbolized in its totality as a centred circle. The dream gives a subtle hint of this, for it is concerned not with a circle merely, but with a circle divided into four: whereas the circle as such would represent a preconscious totality, the division into four symbolizes a conscious and differentiated totality. Totality is not yet realized — if indeed it can ever be — but the direction is clearly given and with it the possibility of at least an approximate realization.

Before I examine this dream more closely in relation to our theme I would like to mention another dream of the same patient's: *I look at myself as in a mirror (but there is no mirror). I see, quite distinctly, a face which is like mine and yet not like mine; more ethereal and spiritual, the eyes full of life and expression. As soon as I realize what I am seeing I am startled and awaken.*[n3]

When the patient told me this dream she said she felt "as if her eye was turned inward". She felt that the "other" face which was like hers was at the same time the face of the self, which she had seen with the eyes of the ego — an anticipatory vision of the individuated personality. This dream is obviously a continuation and variation of the first dream, which likewise pointed to the ideal identity of ego and self, empirical personality and *homo totus.*

If we now come back to our basic question of how to define "meaning", it seems to me that these two dreams give the pattern, the "ground plan", of the experience of meaning. In both dreams — and I would like to remark that they are typical dreams and not isolated occurrences — the dreamer experiences the integral relationship of the personal ego to the transpersonal self. In this relationship the personal ego, because of its crucial importance as the vehicle of the experiencing consciousness, becomes what I have called a "personal self". However little the psychic totality, the *homo totus,* is realized on the empirical plane, the experience of the fundamental identity of personal ego and transpersonal self nevertheless gives our lives substance, direction, and meaning. We can thus say that "meaning" resides in the experience that the individual personality is included within a suprapersonal totality; that it occurs when the ego finds itself to be the reflection and partner of the self. Jung repeatedly emphasizes this when he speaks of the self as the archetype of order and meaning, and Gerhard Dorn expresses the same thing as the "union of the whole man with the *unus mundus*".[19]

Accordingly, in our psychological content something has

meaning when it proves to be an organic part of an ordered whole, when it gives rise to the incontrovertible feeling of a supra-personal order, of being directed toward a goal, of fulfilling a pattern — or, to put it in personal terms, when it makes a constructive contribution to the experience of my life's numin-osity.

Now although this implies that what has meaning for me does not necessarily have it for somebody else, the numinosity of the experience nevertheless reveals an archetypal reality in which every one of us has a share, no matter what particular segment of reality has revealed itself to him. In the numinous, transpersonal character of the experience resides its more than subjective significance. There is an archetype of meaning as such, and even when the meaning seems to be highly subjective, the experience still remains a general human possibility and a constituent element of all humanity.

Another important point is that although the ego is the experiencer and interpreter of meaning, it is at the same time freed from its isolation as a purely rational centre of conscious-ness. Through the experience of the integral relationship of the personal ego to the transpersonal self, or, to use Neumann's term, of the ego-self axis,[20] of the unitary reality, the split between subject and object, the individual and the suprapersonal, is abolished. In the process an "equilibrium" is established "between the psychic ego and non-ego".[21] It is, ultimately, a religious experience in which the ego functions as the subject and organ of the numinous. It is this fact which I was trying to express when I said that in partnership with the transpersonal self the ego becomes a "personal self", or we could say that the ego as personal self is an empirical actualization of the transpersonal self.[n4] Jung expressed this in the great work of his old age, the *Mysterium Coniunctionis*, when he remarked that because of the crucial importance of consciousness the ego could be used *pars pro toto* for the self.[22] In this sense it is no longer an isolated and rationalized ego but an ego that forms an integral part of a psychic totality, and hence of a cosmic totality. This numinous experience was anticipated in both dreams and is inextricably bound up with the experience of meaning.

But here we must go a step further if we want to do justice to the experience of meaning in a deeper sense. If we recall the second dream, where the dream ego saw itself, or its self aspect, in the non-existent mirror, we must consider the possibility that this vision of the self is not just a projection of the inner self but has a reality of its own. Further, in the dream the mirror does not exist, so that the two faces, the ego face and the self face, confront one another as dream realities having the same value. Though we may say that the dream ego saw the self in projection the possibility nevertheless exists that the face of the self was the "true" reality, and that it was the self that was gazing at the ego. In other words: even though our conscious premises incline us to assume that the ego was the reality that beheld the self in a dream, it would be equally possible to say that the self in *its* dream caught a glimpse of the ego. We would then have to consider the somewhat dizzying possibility that a suprapersonal self dreams our ego and by that very fact creates it. For although we regard the ego as real, and hence as the starting point for our knowledge of ourselves, we could just as well start with the self, with a transcendental subject of cognition, which through successive acts of self-realization and self-representation comes to "recognize" itself as the ego, and so creates it by these acts of cognition. Might it not be that we are all figures in the dream of a Vishnu, projections and materializations of his selfhood, as is told in the myth of the Indian sage Markandeya? The legend tells how Markandeya, after wandering around for eons in the body of Vishnu, accidentally fell out of the mouth of the sleeping and dreaming god. Then, for the first time, he saw the god, as big as a mountain, and when in amazement he started to ask: "Who are you?" he had already been swallowed again and was back in the body of Vishnu, thinking that what he had seen was but the figment of a dream.[23] Similarly, *we* may experience the self as a dream vision, whereas in reality *it* may dream us, like Vishnu in the form of Narayana, "the Primeval Cosmic Man, the source of the universe".[24] The fact that the name Narayana means "son of man",[25] and that for all his pre-existent reality and eternally creative power he is only actualized by the questioning and self-reflection of his creature man — this is an expression of the true dignity of human existence and human knowledge.

And here we come back again to the question of meaning. If we take the experience of it as an archetypal content, then it consists in the confrontation and coincidence of ego and self. We must leave it an open question whether it originates in an act of cognition on our part which creates the world, or in the dream of a Narayana, who creates man and in whom man dreamingly experiences himself. Here our logical thinking leaves us in the lurch, for we have reached the limits of rational reflection and only the paradoxical imagery of myth can lead us further. The final logical formulation that is possible for us, even though it presents difficulties, would be to take the meaningful relationship of personal ego and transpersonal self as a synchronistic phenomenon which, in Jung's words, postulates "an *a priori* meaning that apparently exists outside man".[26]

Needless to say, we very rarely experience meaning at such a depth. I only wanted to show in what deep-lying substrata the experience of meaning is rooted. What we generally experience as meaning is a partial cognition, a partial disclosure which happens to be accessible to us, so that as a rule we take in only isolated aspects of the meaning of a given situation. To give a practical example, we need only think of the basic fact of human relationship to see how an experience that is an integral part of man and springs from his deepest nature runs the whole gamut of intensity and meaning.

I have taken advantage of the many dimensions of the word "meaning" in order to circumambulate it, so to speak. I began by speaking of the meaning of neurotic symptoms, that is, the meaning *of* something, but afterwards I set out to discuss the experience of meaning as such. In a further stage of my circumambulation, I would like to discuss the meaning of the analytical relationship and see what it can contribute to the experience of meaning in general.

It was with this theme in mind that I mentioned the example of human relationship. For although, as I said earlier, it is through the individual experience of meaning that the ego feels itself an integral part of a cosmic whole, we must, for the sake of completeness, also consider the interhuman situation, the concrete relationship between "I and You". Even though the question of meaning in psychotherapy is answered in the individual's experience of meaning, this answer itself becomes questionable without an experience of meaning such as is possible ónly between man and man. For this reason the question of meaning in psychotherapy is intimately connected with the relationship between patient and analyst, as we find it expressed in the transference and countertransference.

Jung himself came to lay more and more stress on the two principal aspects of analysis: the inner, subjective process of integration, and the objective process of relationship, which can be experienced only with a human partner.[27] If the experience of meaning is to be anything like complete, a human relationship is essential. The hermit in his meditations may have the profoundest illuminations about the meaning of the world, and yet the meaning of his own bodily existence and reality escapes him. Even so dedicated a hermit as the great Tibetan ascetic Milarepa says that the man who strives for his own individual fulfillment follows the lower path, while he who devotes himself to the welfare of others follows the higher path.[28] In any true experience of relationship, in the encounter between man and man, the outside and the inside are inseparably connected with one another: it is impossible to say which is the more important — the experience of the partner, or that of the inner symbolic figure (anima or animus). Both have their necessary place in human life and complement one another by their mutual symbolic significance.

Every genuine relationship is a numinous process that reaches down to the deepest transpersonal, archetypal levels. Relationship means experiencing the world in the other person as an opposite and as a partner, and thus as the other pole of the fundamental bipolarity of psychic experience. It is no more possible to experience a relationship in the abstract than it would be to know what it means to stand under the starry sky at night, or listen to a Bach organ concert, without having experienced those things in reality, concretely, and in person. Concrete participation, "interest" in its literal sense of *inter-esse*, "to be between or among", is indispensable for a real experience of the

starry sky, of music, or of human relationship. And it is precisely
this *inter-esse* that is forced by the analytical situation upon the
patients, who very often have not dared expose themselves to the
experience of relationship, whether it be physical or spiritual.
The meaning of relationship as an opening of themselves so that
the numinous forces can flood through them, as a surrender to a
greater unity transcending the ego, has got lost or been blocked
for them, and with it the meaning of human companionship and
human trust. What these patients are driven to act out in reality
is the general human problem of isolation due to the loss of a
ritual community. Their neurotic isolation makes them at once
the victims of their time, and, through their conscious sufferings,
the forerunners and trail breakers of a new order.

It is of decisive importance that the inner dynamics of the
analytical process lead almost of necessity to an unusually intense
relationship. It pursues its course irresistibly, however much the
patient may struggle against it and however much the analyst
would like to avoid the tribulations and crises of the transference
and countertransference. This happens with all the greater
intensity the less the patient is related to another person in his
ordinary life. Little as the transference relationship can be
compared with any other form of relationship, it forces him for
that very reason to commit himself fully to the *opus*, just as it
obliges the analyst to give genuine answers.

At the same time the analytical relationship is the most
paradoxical it is possible to imagine, so much so that it often
seems to border on the unendurable or the meaningless. This is
shown first of all by the fact that the person of the analyst is only
of indirect importance. If we disregard the relatively rare cases in
which the patient and analyst prove to be two incompatible
quantities, there is from the start a fair possibility that a
relationship will be established between two completely, or
almost completely, unknown personalities. Although the choice
of an analyst is very often dependent on external circumstances,
it can regularly be observed how, despite this initial strangeness,
the person of the analyst soon becomes the focus of the most
intense interest, and how the patient's fantasies move more and
more in this direction. The odd thing about it is that all these

feelings which seem so intensely personal would in all likelihood have been constellated in exactly the same way had the patient picked another analyst. As far as personal-infantile contents are concerned, such identical projections can obviously be explained by the neurotic situation of the patient. But beyond this there are constellated transpersonal archetypal contents, and their analysis shows time and again that the patient's emotions, however intimate and personal their manifestations may be, refer to the impersonal, archetypal substratum of the analytical relationship.[29] In other words, however much the analyst appears to draw the constellated emotions to himself, he is in reality only the foreground for an archetypal figure, an archetypal partner against whose anonymity the patient learns to break the chains of his fear and to embark upon the venture of love. He can do this because behind all his personal fears and deformations he too finds himself addressed as an archetypal partner, and as a result of this archetypal partnership his personal problems can be resolved and the meaning of human relationship be experienced in a positive sense.

It is just for this reason that concretizations of the transference relationship, which the analyst may slip into because of his own unconsciousness, work out so negatively. For whenever he gets involved in a concrete love relationship he has been unfaithful to his own archetypal function, has become a human being like any other, and is no longer capable of solving the patient's neurotic problem by the numinous power of that function. The transference relationship demands that the analyst be continually alert and conscious of his own complexes and unresolved problems. Strictly speaking, what is required of him is a selfless Eros, which is directed only toward the patient and his *opus*. He is, as it were, the safe *temenos* within which the patient's affects can be symbolically worked out, whatever their nature. However senseless and unendurable the relationship may seem to the patient at first, however painful and humiliating he feels his unrequited erotic wishes to be, this *temenos* nevertheless forms the alchemical *krater* in which the *aurum non vulgi* is purged of its dross. It is a magic circle for the weaving of an intense human relationship in which isolation and loneliness are overcome, and also for the

symbolic course of the *opus contra naturam*, in which concreteness of expression is transformed into the inner image of the
coniunctio.

This Eros, called by Plato "the desire and pursuit of the
whole", in which after many sufferings the patient participates as
consciously as the analyst, is the true answer to the question of the
meaning of the analytical relationship. In the image of the
temenos, Eros is the projection of the self — a *complexio oppositorum* of love and hate, light and darkness, affirmation and
negation — on the interhuman plane, so that the analytical
relationship becomes a reflection and symbol of the world and of
concrete human relationships in general. Without real relationship to the other person, without the opposite pole of love,
individuation and integration remain vanity and illusion. Only in
relation to our fellow man does the archetypal polarity of the
psyche assume concrete form; only with a human partner will
man's inborn experience of his own individuality become a
genuine reality which he has won for himself. The meaning of the
analytical relationship, its dignity, lies in its being the sheltering
and nourishing vessel of the alchemical process, whose goal is the
experience of the individual's uniqueness and of his commitment
to others, which together constitute the meaning of human
existence.

With this I come to the end of my remarks. I started with the
two basic facts of our time. The first was the hypertrophy of ego-
consciousness and the increasing rationalization of life, which
lead to isolation and mass-mindedness.[n5] The second was the
practical responsibility, unknown in any other age, which is laid
upon man by the incalculable discoveries of modern physics and
which, by the look of things, is too heavy for him.

By a compensation of fate, it is the discovery of the unconscious
that makes a wholly new answer appear possible in this precarious
situation. Truly, in modern depth psychology we have before us a
highly impressive "smaller than small, bigger than big!"[30] This
unconscious, which cannot be imagined or represented, which
defies all definition, which consists of nothing but contradictions
and paradoxes and is rejected by the rational intellect as "non-
sensical" — does there not lie in its depths, once our consciousness
has recognized and acknowledged its vastness, the hidden power

which is our greatest and perhaps our only hope? Is not the process of confronting it and coming to terms with it possibly the true answer of our time to our present conflicts, the answer by which our time can discover its own meaning, or any meaning at all? For in the numinous experience of the unconscious a man is in the grip of a power greater than himself, the conflict between faith and knowledge is resolved in the uniting symbol and meaning once more becomes a fact that can be experienced.

Is it not conceivable that a future age will look back on our age of atomic fission and fusion in exactly the same way as Jung's researches have taught us to look back on alchemy? Just as in alchemy a dawning stage of consciousness projected itself into matter, so the processes of nuclear fission and fusion may ultimately be the correlates of inner processes of fission and fusion which, because of their unconsciousness, are projected into matter and, so to speak, acted out in it. And may we not hope — perhaps against all hope — that in these intangible energic processes there may also be projections of completely new psychic potencies, whose very newness makes them so explosive? May it not be that we have here still untapped sources of energy for a new synthesis and a new assignation of meaning?

None of us can supply the answer; but the main ground for hope, based on the actual experience of psychotherapy, is the confession of faith in the creative, healing powers of the psyche, the assigner of meaning.

Perhaps what we are witnessing today is a fateful race between the forces of destruction symbolized by the hydrogen bomb, and the constructive powers of the psyche, for the most part still latent and waiting to be roused. Psychotherapy may have to play a vital role in this conflict. It gives us an instrument which, slight and insigificant though it seems to be, makes it possible to transform the forces of destruction into those of creation. Thus analysis, a tiny and apparently helpless factor when measured by world events, may yet contribute to building the bridge that will lead us across the abyss to a new and regenerated humanity, one which finds its meaning in a true humanism, in a genuine relationship of man to man which is rooted in man's relatedness to his own psyche, itself rooted in unfathomable depths.

Translated from the German By F.R.C. Hull

REFERENCES

1 CW 15, par. 131

2 Ibid., par. 130

3 Wilhelm Worringer, *Abstraction and Empathy* (London 1967), p.13

4 Ibid., p.14.

5 Ibid., p.15.

6 Ibid., p.19.

7 Paul Klee, "Notes on my First Forty Years", *The London Magazine*, July 1961, p.72

8 Werner Haftman, *Painting in the Twentieth Century* (London, 1960), Vol.I, p.167f.

9 Ibid., p.122

10 Ibid., p.120

11 *Memories*, pp.250f, 280f.

12 *Bericht über das Seminar von Prof. J.W. Hauer* (privately pub., Zürich, 1932), p.146. Now in *Spring* 1976, (New York), p.30

13 CW 14, par. 670, 673

14 Robert E. Hume, *The Thirteen Principal Upanishads*, (London, 1934), pp.284ff.

15 CW 7, par. 231

16 CW 13, par. 464

17 Gerhard Adler, *The Living Symbol* (New York/London, 1961) pp.95f

18 CW 12, par. 126

19 CW 14, par. 760

20 Erich Neumann, "The Psyche and the Transformation of the Reality Planes", *Spring* 1956 (New York).

21 CW 16, par. 395

22 CW 14, par. 133

23 Heinrich Zimmer, *Myths and Symbols in Indian Art and Civilization*, (Princeton, 1947), pp.38ff

24 Ibid., p.44

25 Paul Deussen, *Allgemeine Geschichte der Philosophie*, 2nd ed. Vol.I, (Leipzig, 1906), p.153

26 CW 8, par. 942

27 CW 16, par. 448

28 W.Y. Evans-Wentz, *Tibet's Great Yogi Milarepa* (London, 1928), p.140

29 Adler, op. cit., pp.216ff.

30 Kaivalya Upanishad, 20; Kâthaka Upanishad, 2.20

NOTES

1 One also thinks of Rilke's words: "ever torn open by our hand/is the god, the

place that heals." *The Sonnets to Orpheus*. Translated by M.D. Herter
Norton. Part II, No. 16, New York, W.W. Norton & Co., Inc., 1942.

2   This experience is echoed in Rilke's *Sonnets to Orpheus*, Part I, No. 13. The
    hitherto unpublished translation by R.F.C. Hull, the translator of Jung's
    Collected Works, follows:

> *Full apple and banana, pear and plum,*
> *gooseberry ... How all this imparts*
> *life and death in the mouth ... I feel it come ...*
> *Look at a child's face when its tasting starts.*
>
> *It comes as from afar ... By slow degrees*
> *do you not grow all nameless in the mouth?*
> *Where words once were is now a pouring forth*
> *of suddenly released discoveries.*
>
> *Give name to what is apple if you dare!*
> *This sweetness, growing more and more intense,*
> *so as, erected softly in the sense*
>
> *of taste, to wake, to crystallize, to clear,*
> *ambiguously sunny, earthbound, here:*
> *what feeling, joy, experience — immense!*

3   Cf. also below "Remembering and Forgetting", p. 138, where the dream is
    being discussed from a different angle.

4   Cf. also Jung, *Psychology and Alchemy*, par. 137: "In the philosophy of the
    Upanishads the Self is in one aspect the *personal* atman, but at the same
    time it has a cosmic and metaphysical quality as the *suprapersonal* Atman".

5   Here I have to mention another phenomenon which also has its roots in the
    loss of instinct: a growing weakness of the ego, as it were a flight from the
    ego, which also leads to de-individualization and collectivization. A hyper-
    trophied ego as well as an underdeveloped one, the one too rigid and exclu-
    sive the other too incoherent and suggestible, represent degenerative forms
    of the true ego which latter fulfils its true integrative function within the
    psychic totality (cf. G. Adler, *The Living Symbol*, p.39).

Personal Encounters
with Jung
and his work

I was 26 years old when I first went out to Zurich to start analysis with Jung. It is not difficult to imagine with what expectations, hopes, and, needless to say, projections, I arrived. I knew that I was going to stay for three months, until Jung had his usual term break, and I was sure that the great magician, the old wise man, the archetype of the self, and what have you, would transform me from a rather insecure and diffident young man into a fully integrated total personality.

I gradually became more and more disorientated and disappointed when I noticed that absolutely nothing seemed to happen — I did not feel any different from what I had felt when I had set out for Zurich. So I left after three months with a profound feeling of disillusionment and frustration. Had it really been worth my while? All the great hopes, all the effort, had been in vain.

But then a very strange thing happened. First my friends, then I myself felt that my whole life, my whole outlook, were gradually changing for the better, that I had got a much better grip on reality, a better understanding of relationship — in short that I had become a different person, much more positive and creative than I had ever been.

Only then did I realize how Jung, by an unnoticeable influence, had penetrated right into the depths of my psyche, how in an imperceptible way of creative passivity he had made myself clearer to myself. Then for the first time I understood what it meant to be in the aura of a deeply integrated person, how the healing radiation of such a person could affect one profoundly without any immediate outward sign.

And then there is another experience which is characteristic of the way Jung worked.

In the winter of 1934 I had gone to one of the by now almost legendary seminars which Jung used to give on Wednesday mornings at what was then the Psychological Club in Zürich. The seminar had been on the "Interpretation of Visions" which had already run for something like 4 years. I no longer remember the exact content of that particular seminar, but it had been one of those days on which Jung had been at his very best and he had communicated a great deal of his unique wisdom and knowledge. The seminar had been full of exciting new ideas and thoughts. I had felt deeply touched and stirred by all that had been said. With me on this morning there had been two close friends; together we left the Clubhouse in the Gemeindestrasse in silence and concentration. I was the first to break the silence, saying: "Today he has truly talked about myself and my crucial problems and answered all my unasked questions." I shall never forget the almost indignant protest with which first the one then the other friend contradicted me: "But no, he talked about *my* problems." — "Nonsense, it was exactly *my* questions he answered." We broke off and looked at each other, realizing that a man had talked to us out of the centre of his being, and therefore from such a level that he included all our individual personalities and transcended them, that we had been in the presence of and touched by a man of true genius.

I have often remembered my experience of that day and thought about it. It seems to me to contain a great deal of the secret of Jung's personality and of a wisdom which far transcended rational formulation. The possibility of talking to people beyond individual frontiers and barriers, of entering so deeply into the layers of common humanity, is only given to the one who himself lives in immediate relation to the sources of life. I have often thought of the present which fate has presented to those who were allowed to meet in their own life such a person of genius.

To us today it may be difficult to imagine fully what sacrifices had to be made, what dangers to be met, before that person of genius had achieved such depth and intensity. For us who enjoy the fruits of the labours of the great pioneers of depth-psychology, it is easy to forget what it must have meant to a Freud to set out on the road into the problems of his dreams — a road, which Ernest Jones in his great Freud biography calls Freud's "most heroic deed" — or for a Jung to expose himself so unreservedly to the powers of the archetypal images as he did. At least we can see and feel something of Jung's courage through his report in his *Memories*. They make it evident what dark nights of the soul, which danger-fraught experiences had to be lived through before the *deus absconditus*, the hidden god, released his creative realizations. In a letter of 1936, not published in the selection now available, Jung writes: "The problem of crucifixion is the beginning of individuation, *there* is the secret meaning of the Christian symbolism, a path of blood and suffering — like any other step forward on the road of the evolution of human consciousness. Can man stand a further increase of consciousness? ... Is it really worth while that man should progress morally and intellectually? Is that gain worth the candle? That's the question. I don't want to force my views on anybody else. But I confess that I submitted to the divine power of this apparently unsurmountable problem and I consciously and intentionally made my life miserable, because I wanted God to be alive and free from the suffering man has put on him by loving his own reason more than God's secret intentions. There is a mystical fool in me that proved to be stronger than all my science. I think that God in his turn has bestowed life upon me and has saved me from petrification ... Thus I suffered and was miserable, but it seems that life was never wanting and in the blackest night even, and just there, by the grace of God, I could see a Great Light. Somewhere there seems to be great kindness in the abysmal darkness of the deity ... Try to apply seriously what I have told you, not that you might escape suffering — nobody can escape it — but that you may avoid the worst — *blind* suffering."

Such an attitude puts a heavy obligation on us who want to be his pupils: the obligation for personal decision. Thus in my own analysis with Jung, about two years along, I dreamt that he had died. I was in his house in Küsnacht, in the ante-chamber of the room where he was lying in state. I was depressed and dejected, and I paced up and down the room; suddenly my mood changed. I felt new courage and determination grow in me and I said to a friend who was with me: "It does not make it better to moan and sigh. Now he has left us, and it is up to us to continue." When I told Jung the dream his reaction was simply: "All right, now you can begin your own work with patients."

This experience of separation, which everybody experiences in one form or another, is without doubt a challenge to accept one's own responsibility and find one's own way. This step into one's own individuality means the end of identification with the great figure of authority; it may even mean that one may have to take a different path. In this connection it is important to remember that today there are left only relatively few people who have encountered Jung personally. To most people Jung will have become alive through his writings or, maybe, through analytical work with one of his direct or indirect pupils. In this lies also the chance and the need for new searching.

Such new possibilities are not just of a personal nature, in the sense of a continuous challenge to oneself, but they also confront us with the need to test and query the discoveries and formulations of the great pioneers. It is truly the essence of great research to create ever new levels of awareness which in their turn become the springboard for future discoveries and the enlargement of the present sphere of consciousness, even though we can as yet hardly discern in what direction any new steps may lead us. I shall return to this point later on.

In the beginning I spoke of the dangers which a pioneer like Jung exposed himself to when he faced the world of the great archetypal images. Another side of this travail is the loneliness in which the genius has to live. When I read Jung's *Memories* for the first time I was deeply moved and disturbed by the immense loneliness which they revealed. This loneliness is manifest also in the continuous misunderstandings which the pioneer has to face. And not only misunderstandings, but reproaches from the side of the collective that feels threatened in its foundations.

One morning I arrived in Jung's house and found him in a bad temper. With indignation he told me that he had been made the scapegoat for the breakdown of a patrician Swiss marriage, the partners of which he did not even know. But was this accusation not perhaps justified in a certain sense? Could it not have been that Jung's thoughts about human relationships in their authentic meaning, about the obligation to inner honesty, and about the right to be seen and treated by the partner as a true individual had penetrated the collective, protective wall of this so-called good marriage?

Jung himself felt this loneliness as a heavy burden. In a letter of November 1960, also unpublished, during the last year of his life, he wrote in a short and uncharacteristic bout of depression: "Your letter has reached me at a time which was the tail end of a series of disappointments ... I had to understand that I was unable to make the people see what I am after. I am practically alone. There are a few who understand this and that, but almost nobody sees the whole ... I have failed in my foremost task: to open people's eyes to the fact that man has a soul, and that there is a buried treasure in the field and that our religion and philosophy are in a lamentable state ... "

Jung's words express clearly how he experienced and suffered from the incompleteness and faultiness of the world's condition. But it is just out of such realizations that the creative spirit helps to shape the character of a new generation.

In what then do I see these great concepts pointing into the future? I cannot go into a detailed account of the more practical and therapeutic discoveries. Let me mention only a few fundamental ideas, such as Jung's typology, so often misunderstood as a schematic pattern of personality, but in reality revealing the dynamic interplay of opposites; or his revolutionary discovery of the psyche as a self-regulating system, based on his description of the creative function of the unconscious; or again his description of the mechanism of projection or of the dialectic relationship of analyst and patient and of the phenomenon of counter-transference; his strikingly new definition of the symbol with its dynamic and integrative effect as a transformer of energy, emphasising a finalistic point of view as against a purely causal one, or still again his discovery of the archetypes of the collective unconscious which opened up completely new vistas into the understanding of psychic processes and for the content of the imagery of religion, alchemy, poetry, and many other subjects. To these there still has to be added the concept of synchronicity as a profound challenge to the assumption of universal linear causality. And finally, as the synthesis of all Jung's ideas, we have to mention his concept of the process of individuation.

One could, of course, talk for hours on each of these subjects. Instead, I want to concentrate on a few aspects of his work which I regard as particularly important in their wider cultural significance. Here I think first of Jung's concept of the *reality of the psyche*, then of the *creative role of Eros,* and thirdly of his emphasis on the *individual as the creative centre of cultural development*, giving human life its dignity and meaning.

First, let us consider the reality of the psyche. My initial dream in my analytical work with Jung brought me into immediate and convincing contact with the factual way in which he approached psychic contents. Just before my departure for Zürich I had seen in a dream a large map of India, a dream-India, with its characteristic great triangular shape. I had landed on the coast and set out on a dangerous expedition into Tibet. There were numerous geographical details on my dream-map which could not be found on any real map. But what did Jung do? He did not treat my dream in an abstract and, as one might have expected, purely analytical, way. Instead he fetched an enormous atlas of the world, and the great master and the rather anxious beginner knelt together on the floor and studied the map of India. So told, it may sound a trivial event; but it made all the difference to me; it went right into my guts and conveyed to me the uniquely real way in which Jung treated psychic facts.

Another example is perhaps even more striking. During an interview Jung was called to the telephone by an urgent message. A patient was in dire distress, in an almost schizophrenic condition of being flooded and swamped by the invasion of powerful archetypal images. Full of terror she told Jung over the telephone how she felt in the midst of a typhoon, tossed about helplessly in her small boat. How did Jung react? All he said very calmly was: "Well, if that is so, you just reef your sails and lie down quietly at the bottom of your boat until the storm has blown over". And it did — the patient survived the crisis safely.

I hope it is not necessary to try and describe further what Jung meant when he talked of the reality of the psyche. He himself has

called the idea of psychic reality "the most important achievement of modern psychology".[1] So far from being a mere epi-
phenomenon or what has been called a Cartesian "ghost in the
machine", the psyche was for Jung in his own words "superlatively
real".[2] In a different context he said that "the world hangs on a
thin thread, and that thread is the psyche of man".[3]

When Jung describes the scientific study of the psyche as the
science of the future,[4] so we may today ask ourselves which
directions such exploration might possibly take. Jung himself was
fully aware of the fact that his revolutionary concept of the reality
of the psyche was still unacceptable to the vast majority of people.
And how few people are even today prepared to acknowledge the
decisive role of the psyche for religion, philosophy, art, or —
especially — for politics, economics and other apparently purely
material areas.

The still predominant lack of understanding of the discoveries
of parapsychology also clearly demonstrates the resistance against
psychic realities. The idea that there exist forces or entities of a
psychic or immaterial nature which can directly influence the
material side of the world, is still anathema to most even though
the discoveries of psychosomatic medicine should have opened a
breach in the wall of pure materialism.

Here one must mention Jung's fertile idea of the coincidence
and. parallelism of psychic and physical phenomena. It could
explain a great deal of what parapsychological as well as
psychosomatic research has discovered. What a revolutionary
idea to talk of the unity of the subject of psychic and physical
research! What courage to venture forth into the dark frontier
areas of psychic existence! And what does science today think of
Jung's important concept of synchronicity which in the long run
points towards a hidden order and meaningfulness of the universe, far transcending purely rational formulation. Does Jung's
so-called and often criticized lack of clarity and preciseness not
spring exactly from this familiarity with non-rational and
numinous processes, hidden to most, from his daring to venture
into unknown and even forbidden territory?

Jung was only too aware of this quandary, but he had
deliberately decided to forego "scientific" clarity for the sake of

psychological truth which demands an "open" and equivocal language, doing justice to the hidden and symbolical meaning of psychic processes.[n1]

Boris Pasternak has expressed a similar view from the poet's standpoint. He says: "I am always astounded to see that what is laid down, ordered, factual, is never enough to embrace the whole truth, that life always brims over the rim of every vessel".[5] And the words of Matisse: "L'exactitude ce n'est pas la vérité", are well known.

Jung's interest in every human phenomenon, every aspect of man's psyche, led him to the exploration of subjects which many people regarded as "unscientific". He had the courage to stand by his experiences even where they seemed to transcend the limits of rational explanation.[n2] For this he has been called a mystic, a philosopher, or even a prophet. But in fact Jung here showed the courage of the true scientist who looks at facts as they are.

To give only one example: I do not know how many of my readers are familiar with or have even used the oracle of the ancient Chinese *Book of Changes*, of the *I Ching*.[6] Jung has written a foreword to the 1950 English translation of the *I Ching* where he calls it "a great and singular book". There he reveals that, having first learned about its practical application from Richard Wilhelm, he had interested himself for many years in the oracle-technique of the *I Ching*. He did so because, as he says, "it seemed to me of uncommon significance as a method of exploring the unconscious".

The great puzzle is, of course, how any book, particularly one originating thousands of years ago in a different culture, can give convincingly meaningful answers. That it does so seems to me beyond doubt. I have long considered the *I Ching* the most expressive symbol for the profoundest content of analytical psychology. It seems to me that whenever one consults the oracle one commits, knowingly or unknowingly, a metaphysical act of greatest significance. Whoever uses the oracle seriously tunes himself each time into a cosmic process which reveals the coincidence of individual fate and universal fate. The oracle confirms the individual as a meaningful particle of the universe and bears witness to his continuous interrelation with its processes and laws. Such interdependence is a testimony to the individual of his dignity and significance; it is a token of his integral place in the cosmos.

Jung has described this interdependence and correspondence impressively in his essay on the "Transformation Symbolism in the Mass" when he speaks of the double aspect of the Mass, its divine and its human significance. He says: "Although this (sacrificial) act is an eternal happening, taking place within the divinity, man is nevertheless included in it as an essential component ... Just as, in the sacrificial act, God is both *agens et patiens*, so too is man according to his limited capacity ..."[7]

We still know so little of the workings of coincidence that each time we meet them we are deeply stirred, as for instance in the oracle of the *I Ching*. Here surely, Jung has opened up new vistas for the future. He has shown the potentialities of human consciousness for further development, pointing in the direction of an ever deeper relation to the pregnant depth of the psyche and its reality. I think it possible that Jung's greatest importance lies here, more than, for instance, in his psychotherapeutic ideas. It seems to me likely that Jung's metapsychological insights will have the greatest influence in shaping the future. In them we have the foundation for a psychology of civilization and culture.

But in all this we should not forget Jung's deep roots in the realities of this world, his enormous vitality, his earthiness and love of nature, his tremendous sense of humour, his antipathy to the misuse of oracles and uncritical acceptance of Eastern teachings — in short, the fact that he was a man of the immediate present and its needs, grounded firmly in the best of European tradition as well as a cosmopolitan looking far into the future.

As far as Jung's psychotherapeutic discoveries are concerned, I believe in an ever growing convergence of different psycho-therapeutic schools in spite of their different and even contra-dictory anthropological images. I believe this mainly because every true therapist is in the long run confronted with the same reality, which is the reality of the patient who has given him his trust. But Jung has pointed far in the future, not only with a new image of man but also with a completely new vision of a cognitive approach to reality which comprises both the rational and the non-rational. When Jung time and again emphasises the scientific character of his work — and it seems to me sometimes over-emphasises it — we can perhaps still see a residue of his struggle with the limitations and misunderstandings of his contemporaries. A fascinating and sad comment on this is how one of the leading English text books on psychiatry treats Jung's work. Apart from mentioning briefly his word-association studies, all the authors have to say about Jung, in a book of over 600 pages, is that "his interest in Eastern superstition and alchemy betrays his indifference towards the scientific attitude"[8].

Henri Bergson once remarked that humanity has from all eternity been surrounded by electricity, but that it took milleniums until man discovered it. Perhaps we can equally say that there exist forces in the psyche inherent in it from the very beginning, but their discovery needed a similar time, the larger part of which still lies before us.

If we pursue Bergson's remark further, we may perhaps say that we are not only faced with inner psychic forces, but that as in the case of electricity we are surrounded by forces which we are still largely or completely unaware of, but which nevertheless exert the strongest influence. Here again we may assume a correspondence between within and without, a correspondence which could do away with the fatal opposition between and separation of subject and object.

What happens outside me has its correspondence within me, and what happens within me is the symbolic expression of the world around me. How far Jung went with his approach to the problem of inner and outer reality is shown by a remark of his that, if there occurred an accident outside his house, he would have to ask himself in what way he himself was in disorder.[n3] And on an everyday level concepts like animus and anima, shadow or projection, when taken seriously, show the profound coincidence of inner and outer events. The woman or the man outside cannot be separated from the image of the inner woman or man, the animus or anima; the negative situation or person outside has an inseparable correspondence to my inner negative side, the shadow, which we experience in our projection on an outer person or situation.

The Swiss psychoanalyst and psychiatrist Ludwig Binswanger has talked of the doctrine of the cleavage of being into subject and object as "the cancer of all psychology",[9] and from the side of physics Heisenberg remarked that "the common division of the world into subject and object, inner and outer world, body and soul, is no longer adequate ..."[10] This is exactly what Jung has expressed in his profoundest writings. Take the idea in art of negative space. This concept signifies that an object is not only definable by its contours but just as much definable by the space surrounding it. In other words, the "outline" of an object is also the "inline"[11] of the space around it. I can draw an object by its contours, but also by the planes or spaces surrounding it. Henry Moore for instance has made considerable use of this means of representation.

Analogously, man is just as well definable by his outlines, his boundaries, as he is by the inline of the cosmos surrounding him. This vitally changes the relation of subject and object, so that inner psychic forces could also be explained and understood as manifestation of outer energies around us. Here we have one of the philosophical problems of perspective as it has been developed in the Renaissance: perspective separates object and subject in an illusory way whereas up until then, say in the paintings of a Cimabue or a Giotto, the unity of subject and object is preserved, not to speak of Chinese painting or Byzantine art.

It is not by chance that the discovery of perspective went hand in hand with the discovery of rational scientific methods. Necessary, inevitable and creative as they were on the way to greater consciousness, they have suffered the hubris of their one-sidedness. Jung has done a great deal to establish a synthesis on a higher plane by his exploration of the non-rational aspects of the psyche. In a letter of 1937 he expressed the interdependence of inner and outer forces: "Action as we know can take place only in the third dimension, and the fourth dimension is that which actually wants to grow into our conscious three-dimensional world. This realization is man's task par excellence. All culture is an extension of consciousness, and just as modern physics can no longer do without four-dimensional thinking, so our psychological view of the world will have to concern itself with these problems …"[12]

Here lies an enormously important and still largely unworked field of research for us. Parapsychology, psychosomatic medicine or the secrets of the *I Ching* are just a few of the areas in which only spadework has been done. But they make one speculate about the possibility that phenomena like the "psi" function of parapsychology, still considered as rather esoteric occurrences, if not as unscientific phantasies, may point to new enlargements of human consciousness in general in the future. All this is supported by recent explorations into the role of the right hemisphere of the brain, with its importance for the non-rational, intuitive, artistic, holistic faculties of the human mind.[13]

Now, after having talked about Jung's concept of the reality of the psyche, let us consider his emphasis on the creative aspect of Eros, the carrier of relatedness and instinctive wisdom. In a way all of Jung's research which occupies itself with the non-rational at least hints at the world of Eros. This is most evident in his alchemical writings in which time and again the fourth principle stands at the centre, the forgotten or lost feminine. The whole area of the non-rational, of the *prima materia* aspect of the psyche, of its *yin* aspect, is deeply connected with Eros. This is nowhere more impressively formulated than in Jung's "Answer to Job", where God's Sophia appears as the principle of the future, as highest authority, that which can revitalize and transcend an obsolescent and rigidifying concept of God. It is no mere chance that "Answer to Job", with its inherent avowal of Sophia, is Jung's most personal and human book. When, in a letter to Erich Neumann in 1952,[14] he sets his realizations (*Erkenntnisse*) i.e. Logos, against his state of being seized (*Ergriffenheit*) in which he wrote the book, and when he calls this state "barbaric, infantile and abysmally unscientific", he expresses his profound and immediate relationship to the *yin* side, to Eros. Here Jung has initiated an historic change of accent, the importance of which we can as yet hardly grasp.

Another side of the problem of Eros is that of personal relationship. The conflict Eros-Logos is, after all, not confined to psychological theory but is first of all of immense personal significance.

Here the problem of Eros passes over into the third area mentioned before, that of the individual as the creative centre of cultural development.

Nowadays it is a commonplace to talk of the gap between man's moral/emotional development and his technological advance. All of us, be it in the personal or professional sphere, are perpetually hit and hurt by the state of disorientation and anxiety in which mankind lives today. Most of all this is a problem of the young generation. The violent excesses of youth, the exaggerated emphases on sexuality, the use of drugs — are they not all expressions of despair and perplexity and alienation which together can be called the syndrome of our time? But there is a different hidden aspect, the inclination towards the non-rational and Eros, manifesting itself only in primitive and chaotic forms because it is so new. "Women's lib", protesting against the degradation of femininity, against the loss of true Eros; industrial unrest, manifestly concerned with material advantages but essentially, at bottom springing from a reaction against the degradation of uncreative work; and last but not least the growing protest of the young generations, they all have their significance positive side — in them we can discern the deep desire and need for genuine values, honest relationships, and total commitment. The hypersexuality of our days expresses the longing for true Eros and the experience of transpersonal powers; the drug craze contains the intense wish for the non-rational, numinous and archetypal.

The young generation expresses the *Zeitgeist*, the spirit of the times, with all its potentialities, problems and dangers. They seem to express Jung's message in a state of archetypal chaos, as it were, still contained in its *prima materia* or *materia confusa* state. One cannot overlook the fact that they are too often lacking the direction of the ego, the control of consciousness, allowing too much play to the destructive side of psychic energy. In the long run the outcome will depend on the role the positive factors will or will not play in their thoughts and actions. But this seems to be a problem inherent in every development which has in itself the germs of futurity and the potentiality for greater consciousness. Dare we forget that we find ourselves on the verge of a new aeon, that Aquarius puts his demands, even though their fulfilment may be accompanied by crises and catastrophies characteristic of every transition into a new era? Need we recall the transition from the aeon of Aries into that of Pisces which destroyed an ancient world and saw the birth of Christ?

I am constantly impressed by the interest of the young generation in Jung's ideas, or in such related books as those of Hermann Hesse, or the *I Ching*; and even more impressed by the seriousness of their searching which characterizes the best among them. Jung's growing influence which often seems to work in a hidden way is difficult to assess. But it seems to me that he plays a world-historic role through the profundity of his ideas. Through them he talks to everybody, to the old who have become concerned about the impasses into which their obsolescent and obsolete attitudes have led a whole generation, and to the young who are facing the same situation, clamouring for change and renewal. This common concern manifests itself most significantly in the renewed experience of the dignity of the individual who in his relation to transpersonal values and in his living encounter with Eros has the chance to build a new and truly human religiosity.

The revaluation of Eros, the ascertainment of the reality of the psyche, the new vision of man as partner in a cosmic process — they all have to be seen in their wider historical context. With them, as with his other discoveries, Jung proves himself the pioneer of transition and transformation, of a new aeon. It is up to us to take true and individual possession of what we have inherited from him.

REFERENCES

1 CW 87, par. 683
2 Ibid., par. 680
3 Quoted in Richard I. Evans, *Conversations with Carl Jung*, (Princeton, 1964), p.17
4 CW 18, par. 1358
5 Quoted from Sarah Ferguson, *A Guard Within*, (London, 1973), p.18f.
6 Richard Wilhelm (tr.), *The I Ching or Book of Changes*, transl. into English by Cary F. Baynes (3rd ed. London/New York, 1967)
7 CW 11, par. 379

8 Mayer-Gross, Slater, Roth, *Clinical Psychiatry* (1st ed., London, 1954), p.17

9 Ludwig Binswanger, "Über die daseinsanalytische Forschungsrichtung in der Psychiatrie", in *Ausgewählte Vorträge und Aufsätze*, Bd.1, (Bern, 1947), p.193

10 Werner Heisenberg, *The Physicist's Concept of Nature*, (London, 1958), p.24

11   I am indebted for this term to Alan W. Watts, *Psychotherapy East and West*, (6th printing, New York, 1972), p.83

12 *Letters*, Vol.1, p.232

13 Cf. Robert E. Ornstein, *The Psychology of Consciousness* (London, 1975); also Fritjof Capra, *The Tao of Physics* (London, 1975)

14 *Letters*, Vol.2, p.33

NOTES

1 Cf. his letter of 1952, quoted above, p. 11.

2 Here the words of a well known theologican seem to be relevant: "Genuine objectivity is the fruit of authentic subjectivity. It is to be attained only by attaining authentic subjectivity". (Bernard Lonergan, S.J., *Method in Theology*, London, 1972, p.292).

3 This calls to mind the story of the Chinese rain-maker which Richard Wilhelm, the translator of the *I Ching*, told Jung. There had been a catastrophical drought in some part of China and the people decided to call in a rain-maker from another province. The only thing the man asked for was a quiet little house where he locked himself in for three days. On the fourth day there was a tremendous snow-storm, quite out of season. Wilhelm decided to visit the man to find out what had happened. When he asked him how he had "made" the snow, the man said he had not made it. But in the country things were out of order, "not as they should be by the ordinance of heaven". "Therefore the whole country was not in Tao", and so he himself was "not in the natural order of things". So he had to wait these three days until he was back in Tao, "and then naturally the rain came". (Jung, *Mysterium Coniunctionis, Coll. Wks.*, 14, p.419, note 211).

Depth Psychology and the Principle of Complementarity

It is an interesting phenomenon that all schools of depth psychology seem bound to develop sooner or later internal conflicts, sometimes amounting to real schisms. The most famous of such schisms are, of course, those between Freud and Jung, and before that, between Freud and Alfred Adler.

Such ruptures can perhaps be explained by the constellation of different archetypes, different aspects of the unconscious psyche, nobody being in possession of the whole truth and for this very reason are both necessary and can be highly constructive. However, unfortunately, absolute truth is frequently being claimed for one or the other "school". In this psychology is hardly different from religious dogma. Jung, in *Psychological Types*, has made a highly relevant interpretation of this problem.

In the following pages I shall try to explain how I understand one particular — and as it seems to me: crucial — aspect of these secessions.

Even Analytical Psychology has not wholly escaped such inner conflicts, although, fortunately, they have not led to any schism or secession. I personally have experienced these conflicts in a particular poignant way. On the one hand my primal experience of Jung's concepts was based on my analytical work with Jung himself and with the unforgettable Tony Wolff, and on the whole atmosphere of Zürich as it was in the early thirties. Naturally they have been the strongest and most formative influences on my work both practical and theoretical; and in addition my own later independent experiences have served to strengthen my trust in what I had learned and what I went through in my analytical work of that time.

On the other hand I have worked for many years, by now over thirty years,[n1] in London where I was one of the founder members of the Society of Analytical Psychology, established in 1945, and the representative body of Jungian psychology. Whereas at first there was no significant clash between my Zürich training and the general outlook of the London Group, gradually the much more eclectic approach of this group which took in quite a few concepts and techniques from psychoanalysis has led to disagreements.

Faced with this situation I have had on the one hand to test my own practical and theoretical concepts very closely, and on the other, I had to try and understand why, what after careful and repeated examination was valid for me, did not appear so to some of my close colleagues. In these deliberations I have come to the conclusion that we have here something more than differences in method and interpretation, that as a matter of fact we have here a basic problem which has to be faced: a problem of fundamental divergences in approach, an epistemological problem of meta-psychological premises. In other words, I believe that too often and too easily the conflict between and the divergence of the original Jungian and an eclectic approach is taken mainly as one of technical principles, thus concealing a much more decisive question of first principles.

In addition, this to my mind mistaken view has led to certain statements in which the Jungian approach has been criticized in a much too narrow way. Thus it has been said that the difference — or misunderstanding — between analytical psychology and psychoanalysis is the difference between "psychotherapy" and "analysis," by which, if I understand it rightly, is meant that psychoanalysis is dynamic depth psychology, dealing truly with the patient's unconscious, whereas analytical psychology is a kind of supporting and relatively superficial therapy. How far this merely technical understanding — surprisingly among analytical psychologists themselves — of the conflict can go has been expressed in a typical statement made at one discussion that one can recognize without difficulty whether an analyst did true "analysis" or mere "psychotherapy": anybody who saw his patients less than four or five times a week and did not put them on the couch was only doing psychotherapy. It seems that to those holding such an attitude an analysis conducted on truly Jungian principles is less "deep" than one conducted on Freudian or Kleinian princi-ples, and, therefore, less effective. One wonders whether protagonists of such opinions have any acquaintance with the revolutionary results which a true Jungian analysis can achieve, with the explosive and transformative powers of the collective unconscious, and the confrontation with its archetypes which reaches down to the roots and can change a person and his life so fundamentally. Maybe some personal experience is missing from which alone the trust in the analytical effectiveness of this approach might have grown. The overt, or sometimes, covert depreciation of Jung's approach has, of course, its opposite in the attitude of some "orthodox" Jungians who still seem to live with the image of Freud which Jung took with him into exile in 1913, and who regard psychoanalysis as dealing exclusively with sexual and infantile problems and thus inferior to a Jungian analysis leading to individuation and to the integrated personality with profound insights. Instead we should accept that Jungian and Freudian analyses have different aims, and that inside their own area each may succeed or fail.

There is in all such tendentious statements a great deal of arrogance which we have to unlearn. The "Holier than thou" attitude is still all too common and there are too many fashionable slogans about such as that Jungian psychology is not "ongoing" or, we might say not "with it". Such modish catchwords remind me of the phases in paediatrics: every few years the latest and final answer as to how to feed a baby is discovered, only to be discarded at the next latest and equally final discovery of some "ongoing" and "with it" school.

It looks as if we have come full circle and as if much of what is hailed as ongoing is in fact simply backgoing, going back to good old solid Freudian concepts and to a pre-Jungian era. Together with this there is all too frequently a slightly contemptuous or patronizing attitude to Jung himself, as if he were rather antiquated, all right in his time, but now, of course, we know much more and much better. Yet to many of us Jung's discoveries are still so full of unrecognized or undeveloped potentialities that he does not belong so much to the past as to the future. When I say this, I do not want to be misconstrued as meaning that Jung has the last word in psychology, and that there is no going beyond him: all through history nobody has ever said the last word, not even the genius. The genius of Newton does not exclude the genius of

Einstein. I think, however, that what is needed is a great deal of modesty and a sense of perspective.

What I want to express above all is my conviction that criticism based on questions of technique, of three or five weekly interviews, of couch or chair, of reductive versus synthetic, rests on wrong premises and faulty experience. I want instead to express my belief that in our different approaches we are confronted with basic patterns and metapsychological premises disguised as technical problems. In other words: it is a question of the inner truth of the analyst and not of his technique.

Let me, therefore, return to what I regard as the crucial problem. When I use the term metapsychological I want it to be understood not in the narrower Freudian sense of speculating about psychological phenomena and investigating them from the dynamic, topographical, and economic points of view, but in the wider and more literal sense of going "beyond" psychology to its *a priori* assumptions and first principles.

It is, of course, quite impossible in the framework of this essay to give anything like an adequate definition of Freud's or Jung's metapsychological premises. I shall try instead to select what appears to me most important in Jung's work, his crucial concern and central point of view. I shall try to be as uncontroversial as possible, although I realize that somebody else might conceivably make a quite different selection and put the accent on quite different aspects of Jung's work.

My task would have been even more difficult without Jung's *Memories*, where he has given a clear picture of his idiosyncrasies and metapsychological premises. To put it as briefly as possible, what emerges is a picture of Jung as predominantly a *homo religiosus* to whom the meaning of man's life was of paramount importance. His critics, on the other hand, have pointed out that many of his conclusions are too vague, that his concepts are too unsystematic, and that they are based on philosophical assumptions, that he was a mystic, and whatever else belongs to that particular brand of criticism.

At the opposite pole we find Freud: a clear thinker, very systematic, with definite technical conclusions, but not interested in the problem of religion which to him is "the universal obsessional neurosis of mankind",[1] regarding questions of the meaning of life as irrelevant to psychology, and personality as too vague an expression to be of much use. I hope that with these few sentences I have been fair, and that I need give no more than these in themselves quite inadequate hints.

In short, Freud had a clear and relatively limited approach, Jung a relatively vague but comprehensive one. Under this aspect both are complementary to each other. In theory it would, of course, be highly desirable to combine both approaches, but, at least in my experience, this is not possible. The focus of interest will be either on concrete data and material facts, or on the problem of meaning and symbolic transformation. Jung was certainly immensely empirical but to him experience went much further than the material data. Much as he was concerned with so-called facts he had to go behind them and interpret their symbolical background, arriving at metapsychological conclusions. His definition of the symbol[2], so very different from that of Freud's, shows the contrast most clearly. It was already highlighted in their first great disagreement: whereas Freud's interest was focused on the biological phenomenon of incest, Jung's was focused on its symbolical meaning.

Perhaps we can define the two approaches very broadly as the analytical and the synthetic, using both terms in the widest sense. If you concentrate on the one, the other goes out of focus; it seems, as it were, to evaporate. The other approach whichever it may be, loses its urgency and definition, and becomes largely redundant. Again, the ideal would be to develop a third, supra-ordinate attitude by which both approaches could be used either simultaneously or consecutively. This, however, seems just as elusive as the totality of the *homo quadratus*, the thoroughly individuated personality, and in the world of hard facts our own attitudes appear so much formed by our conscious or unconscious premises that we cannot shed them, but must approach the patient and his material always under a particular aspect. The basic attitude of the analyst is much more constant, consistent, and alas, weighted than we care to admit. This will also explain why discussions among analysts are frequently such hopeless propositions. I cannot go here into the fascinating question of what produces these differences in pattern and approach, whether it be a matter of constitution, of experience, of national characteristics such as English positivism and German intuitionalism, or whatever else. A passing and intuitive remark Jung once made to me is of relevance here: when we were discussing why so many Jews had gone to Freud and others had come to him he said: "The Talmudists go to Freud, the Cabbalists come to me".

However that may be, the fact of virtually exclusive alternatives appears to me decisive. It seems to me that however we may try to avoid one-sidedness and limitations, and however often we may delude ourselves into believing that we have succeeded, we have nevertheless made a fairly exclusive choice of approach and interpretation, and hence of evaluation and a system of values.

The course of an analysis is a kind of *Gestalt*, a process following a certain direction and obeying certain laws, and once the process is inaugurated in a certain way, *Gestalt* and direction seem to be more or less fixed. This explains why such wide attention has been paid by analysts to the content of the first interview: it is very often, if not always, decisive for the future course. Possibly one can have different approaches in different analyses one conducts and with different patients, but I doubt if the analyst's own image of what is the right course, based on his own conscious or unconscious premises and his personal equation, ever really allows a sufficiently wide and basic variation. As I have pointed out, what matters is the fundamental attitude which seems to have almost the character of a *Weltanschauung*, rooted as it is bound to be, in certain concepts and convictions belonging to the dark field of metapsychological premises.

This mutual exclusiveness seems to me to have its parallel in modern physics. I am thinking here of the so-called principle of complementarity, a term introduced in 1928 into quantum theory by Niels Bohr. C.A. Meier performed the great service of publishing in 1935 the first study on the relationship between modern physics and modern psychology.[3] Later Jung used parallels between the two in his important essay "On the Nature of the Psyche"[4] and, of course, in his work on synchronicity. I shall make use of some of the material although the aim of this paper is different from either Meier's or Jung's who have both used the principle of complementarity to explain the relationship between conscious and unconscious. In addition I am greatly obliged to Aniela Jaffé's book *The Myth of Meaning*[5]

According to the principle of complementarity it is impossible in an experimental situation to exclude the effect of the observer on the experiment; in other words the experimental situation does not consist only of the observed object but equally of the observing subject. On the basis of this situation the German physicist Pascual Jordan, one of the leading figures in the development of modern quantum physics, has said that according to Niels Bohr there exists "a complementarity between the clarity (*Deutlichkeit*) and the right (*Richtigkeit*) of a statement, so much so that a statement which is too clear (*deutlich*) always contains something "false".[6] In order to avoid false statements one has to avoid being too precise or distinct.

The paradoxical situation of complementarity between precision and correctness has a direct parallel in psychology. The fact is that in psychology too we can aim either at maximal precision and clarity, or at correctness but not at both at the same time. Jung himself was clearly aware of this difficulty as his letter of 1952, quoted above, in the essay on "Basic Concepts of Analytical Psychology", clearly shows. And much later on, in *Mysterium Coniunctionis*, he says that "unequivocal statements can be made only in regard to immanent objects; transcendental ones can be expressed only by paradox".[7]

To sum up, it can be said that Freud's approach is rational, "scientific", as it were, if we use the word scientific in a narrower sense as in the term "natural science". That is, its opposite would not be an unscientific but a non-rational approach, as Jung's can easily be understood to be. Freud's scientific rational approach is wedded to closely circumscribed facts, whereas Jung's non-rational, total approach would coincide with an interest not primarily focused on close factual observation but on the symbolic interpretation of facts and on the intuition of an image of totality. We might also coordinate a quantitative factor with Freud and a qualitative factor with Jung. Equally, "matter" seems to belong to the one, "spirit" to the other — the terms matter and spirit being used, of course, symbolically speaking and without any value judgment. In any case I think we can say that factual observation on the one hand and intuition of the total image on the other stand in the same relation as Jordan's clarity and rightness: facts give a precise picture of the situation but lack the realization of its non-rational totality; intuitive perception of the total image gives a much more adequate and "right" picture but lacks definition and clarity. The one might be called a realistic-factual attitude, the other symbolical.

In this connection I want to mention the simile of the spectrum which Jung used in "On the Nature of the Psyche".[8] There he distinguishes between the location of instinct at the infra-red end, and of the instinctual image at the ultra-violet end of the spectrum. This distinction seems to me parallel to a causal/ concrete interpretation and a teleological/symbolic one. An interpretation focused exclusively or mainly on the actual physical data would belong to the infra-red band of the spec-trum, an interpretation focused on the archetypal image of the same data would belong to the ultra-violet band. To me at least this seems the meaning of Jung's words when he says that whereas red would be the colour suitable to express instinct, and blue suitable to express spirit, violet — a combination of red and blue, of instinct *and* spirit — would express the "paradoxical quality of the archetype". Equally significant are his words that "the realization and assimilation of instinct never takes place at the red end, i.e., by absorption into the instinctual sphere, but only through integration of the image which signifies and at the same time evokes the instinct, although in a form quite different from the one we meet on the biological level". I hope I interpret Jung rightly when I understand this as meaning that only through becoming conscious of the archetypal image can instinct become a constructive agent in individuation, or, to apply it to therapy, only by making the archetypal substratum of a neurotic complex conscious can the complex become constructively integrated.

The lack of definition and clarity and the desire for precision and distinctness could explain the negative reaction of some psychologists. After all, nothing is as clearly definable and identifiable as an actual fact whereas the archetype is by definition non-perceptible, irrepresentable and hypothetical.

Mother's good or bad breast is a so much more tangible fact than the archetype of the nourishing or devouring mother. The archetype can only be deduced from the manifestation of archetypal images on the conscious plane, and these can best be expressed in metaphors called symbols. And symbols themselves are, according to Jung, only the best possible formulation of a relatively unknown thing. Here again we can see the two basic approaches of Freud and Jung: definition and clarity on the one hand and rightness and inclusiveness on the other. It would explain Freud's closed system in contradistinction to Jung's open system. Equally Freud's clear, precise style and Jung's, much more artistic and equivocal, would fall into place considering that Freud's system and aim are rational, logical and limited, Jung's non-rational, religious, aiming at meaning and at a wide but imprecise image of wholeness. However else could we understand Jung's words: "As understanding deepens, the further removed it becomes from knowledge".[9]

Here I want to avoid a possible misunderstanding: I do believe that an analyst can and has to learn from other approaches than his own, and that he can add to and modify his technique. Thus each school or approach can develop and benefit from any other as indeed happens all the time.[n2] I myself am fully aware how my own technical approach and instrumentarium have changed and developed over the years. But I am still convinced that all the time we are faced with different and mutually exclusive possibilities of interpretation, and basic attitudes to the material we are presented with. Our own attitude and reactions, our metapsychological premises not only make a decisive difference to the evaluation of the material but even stimulate or prohibit its emergence. It is not a question of what material is present, but what we focus our attention on and, as I have pointed out, it is my contention that in spite of all possible modifications our focus is largely predetermined and much more fixed and selective than we like to admit. I shall return to this point later. A landscape is what it is, a total image, but it will nevertheless present and reveal completely different meanings to the tourist, the mining-contractor and the painter. Ideally we should have a complete image but, in fact, we are bound to select.

Here I am only repeating what Jung expressed when he drew attention to the importance of the personal equation of the analyst. Equally, the statement mentioned above of the effect of the observer on the experiment in physics only confirms Jung's observations. The problem is even more complicated by the generally accepted fact that the analyst's attitude influences the psychological material both in the sense of what is coming to the surface and how it is understood. The well-known observation that Freudian patients produce Freudian material and Jungian patients Jungian material is not to be explained by suggestion and suggestibility, but by the focus of interest and the ensuing selection.

This is also expressed in the finding of modern physics mentioned earlier that the effect of the observer on the experiment has to be taken into account, that the observer himself changes the observed fact, and that observer and experiment form a total situation in which both variables influence each other to such an extent that any objective understanding of physical phenomena becomes impossible. From a different angle Jung has formulated this, saying: "Between the conscious and the unconscious there is a kind of "uncertainty relationship" because the observer is inseparable from the observed, and always disturbs it by the act of observation".[10] Analysts know only too well that a parallel limitation of objective understanding exists also in the analytical situation. Again, Jung realized this many years ago when he insisted on the interaction of analyst and patient. This observation has been elaborated upon under various aspects by a number of analytical psychologists, and also by analysts of other schools.

I do not, of course, exclude the possibility of the analyst changing his attitude and approach. I believe, however, that for one thing such a change is fundamentally not a temporary technical adjustment to the needs of a particular situation, but a far reaching change of attitude due to some crucial experience of the analyst, and thus a change in his basic premises and his whole metapsychological pattern. For another, since such change is a change in the whole system, it would again be relatively exclusive of the other side which may very well have been his previous approach.

A statement made by Prof. Pauli, the well-known physicist and Nobel Laureate, seems relevant to this issue. In a paper on the "Biological and Epistemological Aspects of the Concepts of the Unconscious"[11] he said that once the physicist in his role as observer has selected his experimental arrangement, he can no longer influence the result of his measurements. He formulated the situation in the following way: "It rests with the free choice of the experimenter (or observer) to decide ... which insights he will gain and which he will lose: or, to put it in popular language, whether he will measure A and ruin B, or ruin A and measure B. It does *not* rest with him, however, to gain only insights and not lose any".[12] Charles de Montet in his book *L'evolution vers l'essentiel* has characterized this dilemma of quantum physics as "the sacrifice and the choice".[13]

I started off with the fact that in depth psychology we find widely different approaches both in theory and practice. I then tried to describe them by such approximate terms as analytical and synthetic, or as focused on actual concrete data or on the symbolic archetypal image. I stated that I do not doubt the value and efficacy of either approach, that I disagree heartily if either side tries to denigrate and belittle the results or range of the other.

Does this then mean that we have to accept a situation in which two widely different and often incompatible approaches are both held to be equally valid expressions or experiences of Analytical Psychology in particular and depth psychology in general? Or do we just witness a process, common to virtually every movement, that it splits up into opposites, a split which is frequently a symptom of vitality and growth? Here I have my doubts, and I want to try to formulate them.

I have just mentioned the problem of "sacrifice and choice" according to which the position of the "cut"[14] to be made by the observer is a matter of his own decision, even though the decision may rest on premises and conceptions of which he may not be fully aware. I believe that this cut, this decision as to what is to be observed and thus gained and what is to be omitted and thus lost, is highly relevant for every analyst. If I try to define the position of the cut I labour, of course, under the very difficulty which I have just pointed out, namely that I have made my own sacrifice and choice. Thus all I am going to say has to be understood from the positioning of my own cut and from my personal meta-psychological premises which in their turn may well have conditioned my own reading of Jung's concepts. With this proviso in mind I want to present certain conclusions arising from what I have said so far.

In his obituary of Jung, Michael Fordham stated that for him Jung's incompatibility with Freud, and the resultant separation, appears a disaster "from which we will suffer and will continue to do so until we have repaired the damage"[15]. To me, from my subjective premises, this seems a basic misunderstanding. If I have tried to apply the concept of complementarity to our psychological situation, it means to me that in Freud and Jung we have two mutually exclusive entities. Much as I respect the attempt to "repair the damage" of their separation, I am afraid that in doing so the essential Jung is in danger of evaporation. It is not just a question of adding certain therapeutic concepts to Jung's system or to Freud's. As I have pointed out before, technique is only a foreground phenomenon, and results achieved by the one or the other technical approach are irrelevant to the crucial problem of fundamental attitudes. On the contrary, in the attempt to blend Jung's concepts with in the last resort, incompatible and incommensurable elements, we are in danger of losing our true identity, a danger of which many symptoms are already in evidence.

To me Jung's fundamentally religious and teleological point of view, aiming at understanding the significance of life through the individual's relationship to supra-personal images and forces, represents an immensely important step away from Freud — I avoid very purposefully the phrase "a step *beyond* Freud". This step was so necessary because in Freud's system there was simply no place for such a point of view. To combine Freud's and Jung's approaches seems to me a task transcending the possibilities of psychology, at least as we know it at present.

A very interesting parallel situation exists in modern physics in the attempt to formulate a unified field theory by which electro-magnetic and gravitational fields could be described in one set of equations. As is well known, Einstein spent many years of his later life on this problem without arriving at a solution, and when Heisenberg in 1958 announced the formulation of such a unified field theory it proved a failure. Maybe the physics of the future will succeed where so far the greatest of its thinkers have failed, and maybe the Aquarian age will lead to a new and heightened consciousness to which an analogous solution of the psychological paradox becomes possible. But so far it seems out of reach.

To mention only one example, I simply canot see how the disturbing fact of the *I Ching*, the Book of Changes, can make any sense inside any Freudian system or approach. From Freudian premises it is bound to appear sheer superstition and a proof of Jung's hopeless mysticism. The famous encounter in 1910 between Freud and Jung when Freud implored Jung never to abandon the sexual theory, "the bulwark against the black tide of mud of occultism"[16] retains its validity however much Freud may have later modified his views. Jung's constantly growing interest in areas on or beyond the frontiers of so-called exact science has a completely different source from Freud's reluctant revision of his views on the role of telepathy in dreams. And let us not forget that Ernest Jones in his great biography of Freud regards even that modest admission as a sign of Freud's regrettable credulity.[17] A phenomenon like the *I Ching* is not just a peripheral problem but is representative of the heart and essence of Jung's approach.

When I talk of sacrifice and loss, the loss is naturally not confined to one side only. Freudian psychology, causalistic, centred on the analysis of transference, and focused on the past and on the concrete material object, stands to lose on the side of meaning, religion, and supra-personal values; while Jungian psychology, teleological, starting from the present situation, centred on the objective psyche and dreams, focused on the archetypal image, is in danger — not unavoidable — of losing on the side of understanding physical phenomena, object relations, and some actual therapeutic insights. Neither is this problem to be solved by confining the one to the first half of life, the other to the second. Although there is a symbolic truth in the fact that the first half of life is so much more concerned with concrete physical objects and actual relationships, and the second half with the inner symbolic significance of relationships and with the meaning of life and death, the problem does go deeper than that. The person of the analyst with his subjective experiences, his faith, his aims, his inner truth, will make itself felt at whatever stage in his life the patient stands just as the latter's personal equation will in the long run be decisive.

After all, it was not just the old Jung who became so deeply concerned with the symbolic meaning of incest or with the borderline phenomena of psychology. Jung himself fought against the reproach of being a philosopher or metaphysician or even a mystic. He fought against this criticism because he felt that he had elevated his approach to the status of true science; but perhaps, also, he was still caught in the idealization of the scientist's image, represented by natural science, so rampant in the first half of the century. These *are* vast philosphical, metaphysical, and even mystical aspects and implications in Jung's scientific researches and results, and to omit them in favour of a Jung who undertook the *Association Studies* or wrote *Psychological Types* would be performing Hamlet without the Prince. Here I want to quote only one passage from Jung's essay on "Synchronicity". It occurs in the last chapter with the title "Conclusion". After talking about "the fact of a causeless order, or rather, of meaningful orderedness" Jung goes on: "The 'absolute knowledge' which is characteristic of synchronistic phenomena, a knowledge not mediated by the sense organs, supports the hypothesis of a self-subsistent meaning, or even expresses its existence. Such a form of existence can only be transcendental ..."[18] Just consider the words "causeless order", "absolute knowledge", "a knowledge not mediated by the sense organs", "self-subsistent meaning", "transcendental form of existence" — who could deny that they open up immense metapsychological problems and vistas!

I realize, of course, how much my own approach is bound to be coloured and limited by my own "personal equation". But perhaps my tentative ideas will help towards some clarification of the problems discussed.

REFERENCES

1 Sigmund Freud, *The Future of an Illusion* (Stand. Ed., Vol. 21.)
2 CW 6, par. 814ff.
3 C.A. Meier, "Moderne Physik — Moderne Psychologie", in *Die Kulturelle Bedeutung der Komplexen Psychologie* (Berlin, 1935)
4 CW 8
5 Aniela Jaffé, *The Myth of Meaning*, tr. R.F.C. Hull, (New York, 1971)
6 Pascual Jordan, *Der Naturwissenschaftler vor der Religiösen Frage*, p.341 (Hamburg, 1963); quoted from Jaffé, L.C., p.28
7 CW 14, par. 715
8 CW 8, par 414
9 CW 10, par. 532
10 CW 9, 2, par. 355
11 In *Dialectica*, Vol.8, No.4
12 Charles de Montet, *L'Évolution Vers l'Essentiel* (Lausanne, 1950), quoted from Pauli, *Dialectica*, Vol.8, No.4, p.286
14 Jung, "On the Nature of the Psyche", CW 8, note 130 to par. 439, quoting Pauli
15 Michael Fordham, "C.G. Jung", *Brit.J.Med.Psych.* XXXIV, 3/4, 1961
16 *Memories*, p.150/173
17 Ernest Jones, *Sigmund Freud*, Vol.3 (London, 1957), p.402
18 CW 8, par. 506

NOTES

1 This paper was written in 1968. In view of what follows it may be important to explain that in the meantime an alternative group has been founded, the *Association of Jungian Analysts* (*Alternative Training*) with the aim of teaching Jung's psychology in an undiluted form. The Association is a group member of the International Association for Analytical Psychology.

2 In order to make my meaning clearer I should like to use the words of the German-Jewish philosopher Franz Rosenzweig on the problem of the assimilation of Jews to their environment. He said that assimilation was a question of declension, i.e. of dative or accusative: do I assimilate myself (and thus lose my identity), or do I assimilate to myself (and thus keep and enrich it). The same clearly applies to my argument regarding assimilating realizations of other schools: I can add to my point of view and enrich it, or my original point of view can become unrecognizable and finally be lost.

Remembering and Forgetting

> While I thought I was learning how to live,
> I have been learning how to die.
> Leonardo da Vinci, *Codice Atlantico*

Remembering and forgetting are such vital manifestations — one could almost say tools — of human existence that without them we would live in a world of chaos. Without remembering we would not be able to recognize any object, person, or situation, and we would live in a senseless and aimless world; without forgetting we would be so swamped by and drowned in impressions and images that we would lose our orientation. Remembering and forgetting are polarities, contrapuntal motifs of the human psyche, two aspects of its total experience, its systole and diastole, and we can rightly regard them as the instruments of human civilization. Remembering enables the human mind to live in history, to hand on the achievements and values of previous cultures, to form and sustain the relationship between past and present, both on a collective and on an individual plane. John Locke has stated that personal identity is dependent on memory, and from this aspect we can say that consciousness is memory and memory consciousness.

What is valid for the individual is equally valid for the collective: a nation, a race, a civilization which loses its memory is condemned to decay and final oblivion. This has happened to many primitive civilizations under the impact of white colonization. On the other hand, a collective which keeps its memory, even under the most unfavourable circumstances, will stay alive and vital. For this latter case the Jews are a convincing example: Jewish identity has been kept vital and creative through the strength of its memory.[1]

This problem of collective, cultural memory is of critical importance for our time: one of the most disturbing symptoms of the time in which we live is that so many of the younger generation try to live not only without any cognizance of their cultural roots, without any awareness of the past, but quite deliberately *against* the past.

On the other hand, forgetting is essential for our sanity — without it we would be suffocated in an infinite ocean of images. There would be no space for new experiences nor for growth based, as it is bound to be, on ever renewed continuous choices. And again this is equally true for the collective, which without a modicum of forgetting would, and often does, ossify and become sterile. Systole and diastole are polarities neither of which must be missed.

The psychologist F.C. Bartlett, in a book entitled *Remembering*,[2] stated that remembering depends on an attitude for orientation which we cannot ascribe to any localized physiological apparatus but which has to be treated as belonging to the "whole subject", or organism, reacting. Such a statement by an eminent experimental psychologist is most significant, since it seems to support Jung's view of the psyche as all-pervading agent and as a totality which, with all its overriding importance, still cannot be localized. Bartlett also stated that every act of recognition, of memory, reflects the preferential reactions of the individual performing the act, whereas conversely in forgetting aversion takes the place of preference.

It is this attitude of aversion which psychoanalysis has dealt with at such great length. It is well known that Freud in *The Psychopathology of Everyday Life*[3] laid the foundations for the psychoanalytic explorations of this area. To Freud repression merely represents an attitude of aversion to the repressed content. He assumes a general inclination "to forget the disagreeable", an inclination in which affective factors play an important part. He defines repression as "the function of rejecting and keeping something out of consciousness"[4] — in other words, a forgetting that was unconsciously motivated.

Jung, in his early writings, frequently deals with the phenomenon of forgetting, particularly in the form of amnesia. He describes how amnesia depends on affective elements,[5] and his doctoral dissertation, "On the Psychology and Pathology of

So-called Occult Phenomena,"[6] contains numerous references to forgetting and amnesia, as do his "Studies in Word Association". [7] Just as important are his references to memory. To mention only one example, in the *Tavistock Lectures* (1935) he defines the ego as a "complex datum which is constituted first of all by a general awareness of your body, of your existence, and secondly by your memory data; you have a certain idea of having been, a long series of memories",[8] and at another place in the same lectures he talks of memories as belonging to the "endopsychic sphere".[9] In a diagram of the psyche presented with these lectures, memory is the first function of the endopsyche.[10]

Finally, a special case is that of cryptomnesia, to which Jung's paternal friend, Théodore Flournoy, had devoted specific attention in his book *Des Indes à la planète Mars*. Jung mentions this aspect of memory in his doctoral dissertation, and in 1905 he wrote a special article about it. He defines it as "the coming into consciousness of a memory-image which is not recognized as such in the first instance, but only secondarily, if at all, by means of subsequent recollection or abstract reasoning".[11]

The crowning point of Jung's inquiry into the nature of memory is his momentous discovery of the timeless memory[12] contained in the archetypal images of the collective unconscious, a memory that comes alive in us foremost in our dreams. There seems no need to go into details of Jung's work on this and related subjects. For this reason we may take a different approach, although even so we shall find constant references to and confirmation of Jung's concepts.

When we talk of memory, of remembering, we are thinking first of all of the act of recognition inherent in remembering. This recognition is the link between past and present, and without it no relationship could exist, no love or hate, no hope or fear. No value or substance would be recognizable. In short, without the function of memory no responsible life would be possible. It is interesting to look at the literal meaning of the English "to recollect" or the German "sich erinnern", which could perhaps be best transcribed as "to refind within". To recollect, to collect what one once knew, to collect together into a new whole — this is what memory is about. A significant polarity exists between the German "erinnern", to refind within, and the German "entäussern", to let go out of oneself. We shall revert to this latter meaning when discussing the problem of forgetting.

The ancients were clearly aware of the overriding importance and power of remembering. Not for nothing was Mnemosyne, the goddess of memory, a daughter of Gaia and Ouranos; of the goddess Gaia, the primordial earth, and of Ouranos, the starry sky; not for nothing was Zeus her lover. Kerényi talks of her as the "cosmic ground of remembering, like a source never ceasing".[13]

It is an interesting question why memory was elevated to the status of a goddess. Here, I think, we are near to the birth of an archetypal image. If I may allow myself some anthropological speculations, I think it feasible that the transition from the palaeolithic to the neolithic age could provide a clue. Palaeolithic man was a fruit-gatherer and hunter, he did not plant nor breed cattle — in other words, he lived a purely parasitic life on the gifts of nature. There was no need but the most rudimentary one to make provisions for the future or to remember any demands of cultivation. But there must have been a gradual shift towards agriculture and cattle-breeding, with an inherent need for a regular rhythm that had to be remembered. In consequence there arose a completely new lifestyle. A new relationship to the land, to a relatively permanent home, must have been the result, in the strongest possible contrast to the unstable, restless, nomadic existence, rooted only in the exigencies of daily life, living from one day to the next.

It may be that at this point prehistoric man was suddenly struck by a new discovery, by what must have been to him the most impressive emergence of a new faculty, of memory. This faculty of memory changed his whole life; a new level of consciousness was reached, and this new power may well have appeared to him divine and worthy of worship. And in our time, through the discovery of the unconscious, have we not even got an echo of such a revolutionary change in attitude?

To return to ancient Greece, it is fascinating to reflect on the offspring of the connection between Mnemosyne and Zeus, the nine Muses; they were the bringers of "forgetfulness of sorrows and cessation of cares",[14] personified in Lesmosyne or Lethe, which is also the river in the Underworld whose name means "oblivion". But the Muses are also the Mneiai — the word is a plural of Mnemosyne, memory. The Greek poets knew that whatever they said "was a repetition of what the muses had told them" a repetition and a memory.

This double name and function of the muses — forgetfulness and memory — shows the polar interdependence of the two. No wonder that near the river of the underworld, near the so-called "Lethaean fields" or "the House of Lethe", near that infernal region, there was also a spring of Mnemosyne, and in Boeotia there were two springs, one called Mnemosyne and the other Lethe. In Boeotia, on Mount Helicon, the Muses had their sacred place and spring. That was where they spoke to Hesiod while he was guarding his sheep, telling him "that they knew both how to lie and how to reveal the truth".[15] Could there be a better picture of the effect of memory which can be deceitful as often as it is true?

But deceitful or true: it is necessary for us to realize — to remember — what vital importance memory must have had for the ancients. No printing or photography, no tapes or television, not even paper for note-taking were there, to help them remember their stories, their legends, their ancestors, or, on a more mundane level, their speeches and orations. It can only fill us with utmost wonder and admiration to think how an Odyssey or an Iliad, the story of a Beowulf or the songs of the Voluspa, were remembered and handed on orally with the greatest fidelity from generation to generation. The power of memory which the bards and tellers of stories possessed is almost unbelievable and certainly non-existent for us. To the ancients, memory was equally a source of wonder. The Pythagoreans taught that one of the proofs of the immortality of the soul and of its divine origin was the soul's possession of memory. Of this teaching we find repercussions in Plato's concept of the soul, a point to which I will return later.

No wonder then that, apart from a natural powerful memory, these people developed special techniques of memorizing, that they invented a coherent and systematic "art of memory", a mnemotechnique. As far as we know this particular art, as so many others, was invented by the Greeks. A trained memory was vitally important, and therefore also a system of memorizing. There is an interesting story about the origin of mnemotechnics reported by Cicero in his *De oratore*. According to Cicero it was the poet Simonides, of the sixth and fifth century B.C., who first devised this technique. To Cicero himself, of course, such mnemotechnics were vitally important as they were to all the rhetoricians, politicians, lawyers, and similar professionals. More than that, to Cicero "the soul's remarkable power of remembering things and words (was) a sign of its divinity".[16]

But to take up the story of the invention of mnemotechnics as told by Cicero, it runs as follows:[17]

"At a banquet given by a nobleman of Thessaly named Scopas, the poet Simonides of Ceos chanted a lyric poem in honour of his host but including a passage in praise of Castor and Pollux. Scopas meanly told the poet that he would only pay him half the sum agreed upon for the panegyric and that he must obtain the balance from the twin gods to whom he had devoted half the poem. A little later, a message was brought to Simonides that two young men were waiting outside who wished to see him. He rose from the banquet and went out but could find no one. During his absence the roof of the banqueting hall fell in, crushing Scopas and all the guests beneath the ruins; the corpses were so mangled that the relatives who came to take them away for burial were unable to identify them. But Simonides remembered the places at which they had been sitting at the table and was therefore able to indicate to the relatives which were their dead. The invisible callers, Castor and Pollux, had handsomely paid for their share in the panegyric by drawing Simonides away from the banquet just before the crash. And this experience suggested to the poet the principles of the art of memory, of which he is said to have been the inventor. Noting that it was through his memory of places at which the guests had been sitting that he had been able to identify the bodies, he realized that orderly arrangement is essential for good memory. He inferred that persons desiring to train this faculty (of memory) must select places and form mental images of the things they wish to remember and store those images in the places, so that the order of the places will preserve the order of things, and the images of the things will denote the things themselves, and we shall employ the places and images respectively as a wax writing-tablet and the letters written on it".

So much for Cicero's story. In modern psychology this faculty of putting two different modes of memory together — here the memory of places with the memory of things — is called "synaesthesia", meaning literally "experiencing together". At this point we may make a big jump, right into our century, to relate a fascinating parallel to the procedure Simonides applied two and a half millennia earlier. It will show that the technique of the ancient Greek was not only sound but rather exemplary.

This then is our modern story. In 1926 a Russian with the name Shereshevskii worked as a newspaper reporter in Moscow. His editor observed that Shereshevskii had the quite unusual power of memorizing verbal messages which he had to deliver to other people. He was struck so strongly by his reporter's memory that he sent him to a distinguished Soviet psychologist, A.R. Luria, of the Institute of Defectology in Moscow, for an examination of his powers. Luria observed Shereshevskii for over thirty years and reported in 1960, after his subject had died, on his experiments with what he called "that most eminent memory man".[18]

Among these experiments were those where he suggested to Shereshevskii "after ten, fifteen, and twenty years to recall certain series of words, lists of figures and formulae. Shereshevskii's behaviour was always the same. He closed his eyes, raised his finger, slowly wagged it around and said: "Wait ... when you were dressed in a grey suit ... I was sitting opposite you in a chair ... that's it" — and then and there quite rapidly he reproduced without hesitation the information which had been given to him many years before. "The observer got the impression that Shereshevskii was rather *reading through* the material than *reproducing* it ..."[19] — in other words, that his memory was based on a visual recall.

How strongly visual it was, and how similar to the technique devised by Simonides, became even clearer when Shereshevskii described how his memory worked. Luria reports: "When we dictated words to him he *saw* corresponding shapes and mostly arranged them in a long row in order not to upset their sequence. Usually he did this, when beginning a 'walk' at Pushkin Square and going down Gorky Street. The reproduction of the series proved to be very simple for him: to him it was only a question of making the same 'walk', and on the way 'reading off' the shapes he had positioned en route" — mind you, after ten or twenty years!

Sometimes this method of an imaginary walk led to omissions, but characteristically these were not lapses of memory but of vision. They occurred, for instance, when "in his imagination he 'positioned' the object in such a way that it blended with the background (for example, a white 'egg' on the background of a white wall) or it was not sufficiently illuminated ('you see', said Shereshevskii, 'it was badly lit by the street lamp and I didn't notice it'), or else it proved to be too small, and then Shereshevskii, in reproducing the series, omitted the corresponding word."

At this point I want to leave the present century and return to earlier times.

Fascinating as it would be to go into the history and development of the art of memory, it would take us too far away from our destination. Only this much would I like to mention: that the art exerted the greatest influence on thinkers right up into the Middle Ages and Renaissance, and even modern times. To mention only a few names: Albertus Magnus and Thomas Aquinas, for both of whom memory is a part of the virtue of prudence, Giordano Bruno, the English alchemists John Dee and Robert Fludd (the latter figures importantly in Pauli's essay on Kepler).[20] Finally, we must name one of the greatest philosophers. Gottfried Wilhelm von Leibniz, whose *Nova methoda docendi doscendaeque jurisprudentia* (1667) contains long discussions of memory in his enquiry on what he calls Mnemonica.[21] These are only a few of the famous adherents and contributors to the art of memory. I could also have opened the list with Aristotle's *De memoria et reminiscentia*, which profoundly influenced both Albertus Magnus and Thomas Aquinas,[22] or with St. Augustine, who pondered deeply on the problems of the soul and the memory, as he recounts in his *Confessions*. Talking of "the fields and vast palaces of memory" he says: "Great is the power of memory, exceedingly great, O my God, a spreading limitless room within me. Who can reach its uttermost depth?"[23] To Augustine, memory was one of the three supreme powers of the soul, the image of the Trinity in man, consisting of memory, understanding, and will.[24] As a Christian father of the Church, he seeks God in the memory, as when he says "Thou hast given this honour to my memory to reside in it"; as a Christian Neoplatonist he believes that knowledge of the divine is innate in memory.

Here I want finally to leave the world of mnemotechnics and go back in history to Plato, who to me seems to have a particular significance for a deeper understanding of the problem of memory. I am, of course, referring to his theory of ideas. In the *Republic*, perhaps the greatest of his dialogues, we find the famous myth of the fate of man's soul. There, he describes in a beautiful simile how man is bound hand and foot in a subterranean cave in such a way that he can only perceive the shadows thrown onto the wall in front of him by objects passing behind him. Only when man is released from his fetters can he see the true objects as such, namely the *ideai*, the ideas, instead of being fascinated by their shadows.

What Plato describes in his simile (or better, in his myth) of the cave is the predestination of the soul. To him all thought is *anamnesis* — remembering, recollecting — of what a soul knew in its pure state.[25] Plato is here near to the teachings of Orphic mysteries, to which the soul was immortal, being both pre-existent and post-existent. There is an Orphic hymn to Mnemosyne which is so beautiful that I would like to quote it in its entirety. It is called "An Offering of Frankincense to Mnemosyne":[26]

I invoke Mnemosyne, who shares Zeus's bed, Queen,
Mother of the sacred, holy, sweet-voiced Muses,
Who keeps memory ever free from maddening fault,
Holding every mind of mortal man in the same dwelling with
   the soul,
Strengthening the mighty reasoning power of mortals,
Most sweet, wakeful, reminding every man

Of whatever thought he may have laid up in memory's store.
Overlooking nothing, rousing every man to consciousness.
But blessed goddess, awaken the initiates' memory
Of the holy rites, and banish forgetfulness from them.

These lines give a truly meaningful and numinous description of the function of memory in its archetypal aspect. What to the initiate of the Orphic mysteries were the holy rites, that to Plato is the world of the ideas, of the *ideai*. They are the eternal, immutable primordial forms of everything which we perceive in our empirical world — be it people, things, or even abstract concepts, for instance, of virtue or of good. Thus the ideas are the only true reality, and the phenomenal world derives from them albeit in an inferior state. In the dialogue *Philebus* Plato states it quite directly: "the soul apprehends the replenishment (namely of wisdom), and does so obviously through memory."[27]

And in the *Phaedrus*[28] Plato describes the transmigration of the soul, which to him is immortal and imperishable. The soul endeavours to follow in the train of a god; whenever she succeeds and thus "discerns something of truth" she will always remain free from hurt. But the soul that is unable to follow a god will "be burdened with a load of forgetfulness and wrongdoing, and because of that burden sheds her wings and falls to the earth". There she is doomed to live in an imperfect body: *soma sema*, the body is the grave of the soul. She has to undergo many transformations until, if the man in whom the soul is incarnated has lived righteously, the soul regains her wings and is allowed, after three thousand years, to "return to the place whence she came" and to regain true understanding. The man, however, who has lived unrighteously will need at least ten thousand years. And to live righteously means "to seek after wisdom unfeignedly", to understand the language of forms passing from a plurality of perceptions to a unity gathered together by reasoning. Such understanding — in Plato's words — is "a recollection of those things which our souls beheld aforetime as they journeyed with their god ... ". This idea is most succinctly restated by Marsilio Ficino, the Neoplatonic philosopher of the fifteenth century, according to whom "the true philosopher strives only to die to temporal reality and to live in the timeless world of ideas" and man is the intermediary between the realm of divine creative ideas and the world, his task ever to remember the former.[29]

All these quotations make it clear that to Plato the memory of the ideas is the commanding factor for the soul's true knowledge. I think that Plato is here expressing a profound psychological truth of which even today most people, and in particular most psychologists, are unaware. It is this: true information is not derived from the ephemeral world of appearances but from the perennial world of the eternal images.

A similar idea is expressed by the Sufi mystic Jalal-ud-din Rumi when he says, "While in form thou art the microcosm, in reality thou art the macrocosm",[30] and, to make rather a leap Schopenhauer, to whom the Idea is the guiding light to all truth, the unit of true knowledge, transcending time and space.

Here we find ourselves directly in the centre of Jung's teaching on the archetypes. They too exist as eternal forms, as pre-existent conditions and patterns of behaviour, and the so-called unconscious is the true source of all knowledge. Thus true knowledge does not come from the ego but from the self.

If we pursue this thought further, it can lead us to a complete reversal of terminology, not to speak of attitude, and ultimately to a new model of the psyche. We have to realize that our use of the term "unconscious" is completely obsolete, based as it is on a positivistic psychology to which so-called unconscious processes were defined as nothing but "more dimly conscious" processes.[31] In other words, our use of the terms conscious/unconscious is utterly prejudiced in that they define the unconscious simply as a negative consciousness. This comes out even more clearly in the ambiguity of the term "subconscious", which has an undertone of inferiority, as in the word "subhuman". If, however, we take Plato's concept seriously — and *a fortiori*, Jung's teaching — it would be correct to talk of the self as the basic and decisive entity; and then we should speak of the ego as "sub-self" or "un-self" or "non-self" and of the unconscious as "super-consciousness". With such a terminology we would, it seems to me, express the essence of Jung's approach to the numinosity of the "unconscious" and that of his hypothesis of "absolute knowledge", and we would do justice to the fact that whatever we experience through our ego is only an echo or a derivation or an ephemeral configuration of the self. It is truly astounding to see how Plato was millenniums ahead of most so-called modern psychology.

How much Plato's concept of a pre-existent source and basis of all knowledge is in harmony with archetypal truth is shown by the fact that his thought is mirrored in other and very different cultural environments. I want to give two examples, from vastly different cultural areas, one from the Kabbala, the other from the Upanishads.

In the Kabbala we find the legend of "The Formation of the Child".[32] It runs as follows: "At the moment of the creation of the child God ordains that the seed of the future human being shall be brought before Him, whereupon He decides what its soul shall become: man or woman, sage or simpleton, rich or poor. Only one thing He leaves undecided namely, whether he shall be righteous, for, as it is written "all things are in the hand of the Lord, except the fear of the Lord ...." Thereupon God orders the angel in charge of the souls living in the Beyond to initiate this soul into all the mysteries of that other world, through Paradise and Hell.... At the moment of birth, however, when the soul comes to earth the angel extinguishes the light of knowledge burning above it, and the soul, enclosed in its earthly envelope, enters this world, having forgotten its lofty wisdom, but always seeking to regain it."

There exists an interesting Hasidic version of this story[33] according to which the angel who extinguishes the light is the angel of forgetfulness, and the vexing question why God created forgetfulness is answered by Rabbi Baruch of Mezbish, the grandson of the Baal Shem, the founder of Hasidism, by saying that if there were no forgetting, man would incessantly think of his death, he would build no house, launch no enterprise. For this reason one angel is ordered to teach the future child in such a way that it would not forget anything, and the second angel is ordered to make him forget. This story shows again the interdependence of remembering and forgetting, how they are twin aspects of a total experience. But what concerns us at this point is the main theme of our legend; that remembering, recollecting, the eternal truth, is the task of the soul. Here again man has the choice to live righteously or unrighteously, although the climate is different: where to Plato the thought of the philosopher — that is, reason and intellect — was the most important tool of man in his search for redemption, to the Kabbala man's choice is a religious and ethical one: "The fear of the Lord", the acceptance of God's divinely appointed purpose.

A similar myth is found in the Upanishads. In the Garbha Upanishad[34] we read of man, having participated in the wisdom of the Yoga, being born under great pain. When he comes into contact with the Vaishnava wind, the wind of the external world, he no longer can remember his previous births and deaths and loses the realization of good and bad works.

Altogether, memory was highly valued in Indian thought. In the Chandogya Upanishad we find a passage where Narenda, the highest representation of Brahmanic virtues, is instructed by the god of war, Sanatkumara, about the sixteen modes of worshipping Brahma. One of the highest modes is memory. The passage goes as follows: "Memory indeed is greater than the Universe; for even if many sat together, and had no memory, they could not hear, nor think, nor recognize, but if they possess memory, they can hear, think, recognize: ... Whosoever worships memory as Brahma, will be able to wander about to his heart's desire, because he worships the memory as the Brahma."[35] And in the Maha-Narayana Upanishad we find this prayer: "He who was in the beginning, before the gods, the master of the Universe, Rudra, the great wise one, who himself saw the birth of Hiran-yagharba, the God may endow us with a true memory."[36]

Here again we can see a profound understanding of the predominance of the self in human experience. Memory is memory of the archetypal foundations; true memory is relating to the transpersonal or superpersonal centre of the psyche — to the self.

The opposite side, that is the negative power of forgetting, is stressed in Hatha Yoga. Here the mythical hero Matsyendranath has become a prisoner of women and is doomed to die. His disciple Gorakhnath, learning of his guru's predicament, changes himself into a dancing girl and sings "enigmatic songs". Little by

little Matsyendranath remembers his true identity; he under-
stands "that his 'oblivion' was, basically, forgetfulness of his true
and immortal nature",[37] and that it was Durga, the personifi-
cation of nature, who had cast the spell of "forgetfulness" on him.

The story shows the same archetypal pattern as the famous
early Christian "Song of the Pearl" in the apocryphal *Acts of the
Apostle Thomas*.[38] It describes how the son of the King is sent
into Egypt to bring back the pearl of great price, how he, enticed
by the temptations of Egypt, forgets his task and the pearl. His
parents, hearing of his fate, send him a letter: "Remember that
thou art a son of kings ... Remember the pearl for which thou
wast sent into Egypt." Reading this letter the son remembers
forthwith that he is the son of kings and brings back the pearl
from Egypt. What is immortality in the Yogic story is here, in
accordance with the different Christian climate, the divine
destiny of the soul, similar to the mentioned difference in Plato's
myth of the cave and the Kabbalistic legend.

To return to India, the "application of the 'Yoga of self-
liberation' is said to reintegrate all forgotten knowledge of the
past with consciousness". It is, as Jung has pointed out in his
commentary on *The Tibetan Book of the Great Liberation*, a
process of restoration, of restitution, the well-known motif of
apokatastasis which "occurs in many redemption myths and is
also an important aspect of the psychology of the unconscious". It
is a "spontaneous reawakening" — or I would prefer to say a
recollecting, a remembering — "of ancestral patterns".[39]

I think we can say with justification that in the last resort every
ritual is an act of remembering — be it the primitive memory of
the mythical ancestors, the Jewish Passover with its remembrance
of the Exodus from Egypt and God's mercy, or the Eucharist with
its memory of the destiny of Christ.

What connects all these myths and rituals is the importance of
recollecting, of memory: remembering opens the gate to the
soul's fulfilment. Here Wordsworth's lines in his *Intimations of
Immortality* come to mind:

> *Our birth is but a sleep and a forgetting;*
> *The Soul that rises with us, our life's Star,*
> *Hath had elsewhere its setting,*

> *And cometh from afar:*
> *Not in entire forgetfulness,*
> *And not in utter nakedness,*
> *But trailing clouds of glory do we come*
> *From God, who is our home ...*

Is not every artist a true "rememberer", trying to rediscover what Kandinsky called the "Greater Reality", or Franz Marc the "inner mystical construction"? Is this Greater Reality, this inner mystical construction, not just the world of the archetypes, to which the artist gives shape in his images? Is the artist not the man who is in contact with a world of timeless transcendence, remembering and shaping, as it were, the time before the soul lost her wings? Is not every true vision, ever act of cognition, really an act of re-cognition? Paul Klee expressed this when he described the circles which play such a prominent part in Kandinsky's paintings as "the dynamic cosmic form, which comes into being when earthly bonds are cast off".[40] And what is true for the artist is true for every truly creative person: he is an instrument of the numinous transpersonal which forces him to remember what the ordinary person seems to have forgotten for ever.

And on a different level, have we not all experienced this strange phenomenon that something that we met for the first time nevertheless gave us the sudden shock of re-cognition, of remembering, of something that feels as if we knew it always? This phenomenon of *déjà vu* is often explained as a precognition — if it is not explained away as an illusion or self-deception. Jung himself gives two different explanations. The one is as *déjà vu* being based on a foreknowledge in dreams or in a waking state.[41] But he also gives a different interpretation which is highly relevant to our theme. In his *Memories*[42] he talks of the feeling of having already experienced something as if one had always known it. I shall return to this problem presently.

Thus the phenomenon of *déjà vu* may express a true remembering on a plane of nonrational reality. Perhaps we can understand it as the coincidence of ego and self: the actual situation reminds the individual of the relevant mythical or archetypal image. Tennyson expressed this feeling in a poem, "The Two Voices":

Moreover, something is or seems,
That touches me with mystic gleams,
Like glimpses of forgotten dreams —

Of something felt, like something here;
Of something done, I know not where;
Such as no language may declare.[43]

William James, in *The Varieties of Religious Experience* says
about these states of "having been here before" that "they bring a
sense of mystery and of the metaphysical duality of things, and
the feeling of an enlargement of perception ... "[44] This "metaphysical duality" we can understand psychologically as the duality
existing between the perceiving ego and the perceived archetypal
background, a recollection of inner experiences, triggered by
what may appear as a trivial incident.

Jung himself reports such a *déjà vu* experience in his *Memories*.
[45] There he describes the impression which a Negro standing
motionless on a rock, leaning on his spear, made on him. In his
own words: "it was a picture of something utterly alien and
outside my experience, but on the other hand a most intense
sentiment of *déjà vu* ... as if I knew that dark-skinned man who
had been waiting for me for five thousand years."

Jung adds another experience of, as he puts it, "the immemori-
ally known", namely when he first observed a parapsychological
phenomenon. Then, again in his own words: "I felt it was
perfectly natural ... because I had long since been acquainted
with it" and he concludes by saying that the world of the solitary
dark hunter had been his for countless millenniums.

Here we find ourselves in the most mysterious recesses of our
psychic life where the spatio-temporal reality of our everyday
existence seems suspended. Here man transcends his boundaries
and enters into infinity and eternity. The timelessness of the
unconscious which in our empirical life is unfolded into the
sequences of time and causality confronts us with its overwhelming numinosity. It is as if a god saw the whole history of the
universe concentrated in one single timeless point of eternity, a
history which we can experience only as disjunct events. But

suddenly the veil is lifted from our eyes and eternity has overcome us.

The timeless point of eternity[46] appears in Indian philosophy as the "bindu",[47] the drop, which is the ultimate point and concentration of power, both negative and positive, male and female within and without, past and future, remembering and forgetting, zero and infinity — the union of all opposites. It is the centre of *jara*, matter, and of *caitanya*, highest consciousness. In it the archetypal polarity of the universe, "producing forever the Maya of the world",[48] is abolished.

These experiences of *déjà vu* arouse the feeling of an unconscious memory existing in us of what was present before, as if scenes and figures of the deepest layers of our psyche suddenly are lit up and spontaneously and unexpectedly enter the realm of consciousness. What else is the experience of the encounter with the animus- or anima-figure outside but a recovery and refinding and remembering of an eternal presence? It has been most poignantly expressed by Rilke in the third of his *Duino Elegies*:[48a]

> One thing to sing the beloved, another, alas!
> that hidden guilty river-god of the blood....
> Not to meet yours, girl feeling him, not to meet yours,
> did his lip begin to assume that more fruitful curve.
> Do you really suppose your gentle approach could have so
> convulsed him, you, that wander like morning breezes?
> You terrified his heart, indeed; but more ancient terrors
> rushed into him in that instant of shattering contact ...
> And you, yourself, how can you tell, — you have conjured up
> prehistoric time in your lover....

and Goethe expressed his experience in the verses dedicated to his great anima-figure, Frau von Stein:

> Ah you were in times gone by
> Surely sister to me or wife.[48b]

Is not in this sense every important and meaningful encounter with an actual person remembering? Are not all numinous experiences, like the one that Jung describes, a profound remembering of the transcendental matrix? In *Answer to Job* Jung says:[49] "As always when an external event touches on some unconscious knowledge, this knowledge can reach consciousness. The event is recognized as a *déjà vu*, and one remembers a pre-existent knowledge about it." Here the German term for "to remember", "sich erinnern", shows its full significance. It can perhaps best be rendered "to find within oneself", and this is exactly what happens in these situations.

I myself once had a most impressive experience, a profound dream I dreamt at the beginning of the analysis with Jung, in the early 1930s. It was as if I went through my whole life right from the beginning through to its end. When I woke up I had a sense of the absolute reality of the dream experience — but I could not remember anything. When I told this dream to Jung he was certain that the knowledge I had gained in the dream was absolutely correct and genuine, but that for this very reason it was equally important for me to forget what I had learned, since one cannot live life with the full knowledge of its future course. Needless to say that this dream impressed me deeply and that I never forgot it. But what is relevant to our theme is that, without any doubt, I must have encountered during the course of my life innumerable incidents, innumerable people, that activated an unconscious foreknowledge. They gave me the feeling of the *déjà vu*, and in these cases, indeed memories became present.

All such memories need an external stimulus to re-enter our consciousness, be they an actual person or a concrete experience. Walt Whitman describes such a situation when "he writes of the live oaks under which he thinks certain thoughts that he cannot remember elsewhere: 'Sometimes I think they hang there waiting'."[50] And then there is the famous little crumb of the madeleine, the tea-cake, in Proust's *Du côté de chez Swann*, which he used to be given as a child on Sunday mornings, and which now makes him remember his past, setting him off on his momentous journey through *La Recherche du temps perdu*, remembrance of things past.

Here are Proust's words, as translated: "... when from a

long-distant past nothing subsists, after the people are dead, after the things are broken and scattered, still, alone, more fragile, but with more vitality, more unsubstantial, more persistent, more faithful, the smell and taste of things remain posed a long time, like souls, ready to remind us, waiting and hoping for their moment, amid the ruins of all the rest; and bear unfaltering, in the tiny and almost impalpable drop of their essence, the vast structure of recollection."[51]

It is not given to everybody to remember one's thoughts with the help of an oak tree or a crumb of cake. We have to be grateful that there are other ways of remembering, given to all of us, though only too frequently overlooked or pushed aside. Nowadays Freud's idea that dreams bring up repressed childhood material is common knowledge, and it would be easy to adduce countless examples from every analyst's consulting-room. But it is not these repressed, and largely infantile, dreams about which I want to talk. Instead I want to quote Jung's dream of the multi-storeyed house, which he also records in his *Memories*. In this dream he found himself in an unknown house with two storeys, the upper one furnished in rococo style, the ground floor in the style of the fifteenth or sixteenth century, and when he searched further he discovered a cellar, apparently dating from Roman times, and, finally, descending still further, he found himself in a low cave, full of remains of a primitive culture.[52]

Jung tells how this dream led him to the discovery of the collective unconscious, a "kind of prelude to *Wandlungen und Symbole der Libido*", the original version of *Symbols of Transformation*. The dream taught him to recognize "passed stages of consciousness",[53] which he could remember through the contents and images of the dream.

There are other dreams of Jung's, pointing to the same experience of "having been there before". I am in particular thinking of two dreams both, again, recorded in his *Memories*. [54] The first dream, one of a series of similar dreams, was about a strange house or annex to his present house, and each time, so Jung says, "I would wonder in my dream, why I did not know this house, although it had apparently always been there". In another version of the same type of dream he discovered "a wonderful library dating largely from the sixteenth and seventeenth centuries". But then came still another dream, which Jung calls "crucial", where he found himself "caught in the seventeenth century, consoling himself with the thought: "Some day, years from now, I shall get out again."

Jung says of these dreams that they were an anticipation of his encounter with alchemy. But are they "anticipations", or could we not rather say that they were memories of a past encounter? Do anticipation and memory meet here in what we might paradoxically call "remembering the future"? I must leave this question open, but it has fascinated me ever since I read Jung's *Memories*.

However that may be, it is important to realize that Jung's dreams were not just the dreams of an extraordinarily gifted individual, but that in a way they are typical dreams, representing an unconscious pattern of dream experience. Thus a woman patient of mine, at the end of her forties, dreamt that she had another beautiful house as well as the one in which she normally lived, and she wondered whether it was right to have one which she used so little and whether the rent was paid.[55]

I think here again we meet with the duplicity of the "memory of the future": the beautiful house is both the image of a pre-existent fuller personality and the anticipation of potentialities and future developments. The two houses show how she lives, as it were, in two worlds, one of which is remote but superior to the everyday dwelling. It was characteristic that this was a recurrent dream which the patient had had during most of her life. All her life she lived with the memory of a richer world and the anticipation of its realization.

In another dream she looks at herself as if in a mirror and sees a face which is like hers and yet not like hers: "More ethereal and spiritual, the eyes full of life and expression." While we were discussing the dream she suddenly felt "as if her eye was turned inward".[56] Here she experiences the duality of the empirical personality and the total personality, as if in the dream potentiality had become actuality. We have a parallel to this inward turning of vision in Dhyana Buddhism, as reported in the *Sutra of Wei Lang*.[57] There introspection or, as it is called, "turning one's light inwardly", leads to the realization of one's "real nature" or "original face".

Here again, I think, we meet with the phenomenon of "remembering the future", the vision and recollection of the pre-existent pattern, the unconscious wholeness, and of the future possibility, direction, or goal.

But how easy is it to forget both aspects of this situation, to neglect the need for remembering both the inherent pattern and the intimation of the future goal. There is in man a *horror novi*, a basic apathy and indolence which resists the difficult task of remembering and fulfilling the challenge of the *magnum opus* of individuation. And still, even here, the psyche very often finds its own way of breaking through this inertia and forgetfulness. One of the paradoxical ways in which this happens is the appearance of a symptom which becomes so intolerable to the individual that he can no longer avoid doing something about it. Many analyses start in this way, and in many cases the symptom turns out to have been the opening up of the path of individuation. Thus we can understand the symptom as the *ultima ratio* of the psyche, as its last urgent appeal which can no longer be overlooked, which forces the individual to remember his most urgent task and to rediscover his "original face".

The dream of a man in his forties may serve to illustrate the problem of what we might call the watchfulness of the self. This is the dream, dreamt after several years of an intense analysis:

> I am with a group. Fast, fierce "flying circular platforms" with sharp cutting edges are flying low, swooping over us with immense speed and immense skill, around our heads, trees, houses, etc. There is one man with equipment (including a gun) on each platform, and these form the shape of a low sloping pyramid. It seems as if they are attacking and yet they deliberately just miss everything. They fly away and come back again.

If one is familiar with Jung's essay on "Flying Saucers" one will have no problem understanding the symbolism of this dream. In that essay Jung mentions the reports of the "intelligent, purposive movements ... superior technical knowledge and ability" of the pilots, and equally that "they did no harm and refrained from all hostile acts",[58] features which we find also in our dream. Most important, however, is his interpretation of these saucers as portraying the archetype of the self. As such they play the important role of regulators and orderers of chaotic states, "giving the personality the greatest possible unity and wholeness". [59]

Jung's interpretation is borne out by the associations of my analysand. He put it in the shortest possible way: "This is a warning that the neglected self can kill, but also that it is always there to remind us of our neglect on the one hand, and of our task on the other."

What in the dream is told with intense personal poignancy attains all the grandeur of ancient tragedy in the myth of the wounded healer. The divine healer is always wounded or ill. The best known example is that of Chiron, the foster-father of Asklepios, and many other heroes who are all afflicted with an incurable wound: for example, Heracles, who is called "alexikakos" and "soter" (warder off of evil; saviour), and suffers from epilepsy, the *morbus sacer*.[60]

Behind this we can see the idea that to be wounded means to have the healing power activated, or even that without being wounded one would never have acquired this healing power. What is true of the hero is true of each of us, and certainly no psychotherapist ever chooses his vocation without being wounded. Jung's own story as he told it in his *Memories* is exemplary. In our context we can understand the wound as the constant reminder of the need for the search for healing. It is the wound which forces us into remembering our incompleteness and which does not let us go to sleep.

Let me then conclude the first part of my essay with Jung's own words: "We should not try to 'get rid' of a neurosis, but rather to experience what it means, what it has to teach, what its purpose is. We should even learn to be thankful for it, otherwise we pass it by and miss the opportunity of getting to know ourselves as we really are. A neurosis is truly removed only when it has removed the false attitude of the ego. We do not cure it — it cures us. A man is ill, but the illness is nature's attempt to heal him. From the illness itself we can learn so much for our recovery, and what the neurotic flings away as absolutely worthless contains the true gold we should never have found elsewhere."[61]

II

Let me now say a few words about the role which memory and forgetting play in the Old Testament. The notion of remembering as the act of an individual is alien to ancient Hebrew thinking. It is primarily a collective, communal act, closely related to the idea of the name. If a man wants to be remembered, then his name, which carries the substance of his soul, has to be kept alive; the power of the soul must be strong enough to be active through generations. For this reason, if a man has no sons he will set up a memorial by which his name, his soul, can be remembered, that is: preserved. In II Samuel 18:18, we read of Absalom saying: "I have no son to keep my name in remembrance: and he called the pillar after his own name: and it is called" — that is: remembered — "unto this day, Absalom's place."

Correspondingly an enemy would want to blot out the name of his adversary. In Exodus (17:14) we read: "And the Lord said unto Moses, write this for a memorial in a book ... for I will utterly put out the remembrance of Amalek from under heaven." When the name is forgotten, the substance it represents is also extinguished.

Even more important: in the majority of cases it is God who remembers. He remembers his people to protect them, to show mercy to them; but he also remembers the sins of Israel to judge them. And the holiest act of the ritual in the Day of Atonement is the extinction of sins from the book of memory. In this sense to remember and to forget are always synonymous with to act, be it as judgment or as salvation; remembrance, forgetting, are equal to objective and concrete action.

This attitude is interesting from the psychological point of view. As I have said, in most cases it is God who remembers. This

raises the question "What remembers in us, who is the rememberer, and who the forgetter in us?" If we transpose the God of
the Old Testament to our psychological plane, we may say: it is
the self which remembers all events and facts arising from the
deep level of the collective unconscious, whereas the ego remembers the data of the personal unconscious.

Conversely, in the Old Testament, where forgetting is concerned, it is usually a case of man forgetting God, of ego separating
itself from the self. In the Psalms we read (9:17): "The wicked
shall be turned into hell, and all the nations that forget God," or
again (50:22): "Now consider this, ye that forget God, lest I tear
you to pieces" — which we can understand as the threat of
disintegration through loss of contact with the self.

God also can forget man for his sins and disobedience. "How
long wilt thou forget me, O Lord? for ever? how long wilt thou
hide thy face from me?" (Psalms 13:1) — the threat of the self
becoming inaccessible to the ego on account of its neglect from
the ego side. But such loss of contact need not be permanent; just
as man can never completely sever his connection with God, so
God will never forget man completely. Self and ego are bound by
stronger bonds than failure can ever destroy.

The idea of the concreteness of the act of remembering as a
commitment to the laws of God is expressed, e.g., in Leviticus
(2:9), where it is said that the "priest shall take from the meat
offering a memorial thereof, and shall burn it upon the altar: it is
an offering, made by fire, of a sweet savour unto the Lord".
Rashi, the most famous of Biblical commentators, living in the
eleventh century, explains this offering as an act by which the
giver is "remembered for good and for having caused satisfaction
to the Lord".

The active effect of remembering is also to be found in the New
Testament. In I Corinthians (II:24-25), Jesus is reported as
saying, when breaking the bread of the Last Supper: "This is my
body, which is broken for you: this do in remembrance of me",
and he says the same when offering the cup as "the new testament
in my blood": "This do ye, as often as ye drink it, in remembrance of me." Here again it is not just an act of passive
remembering but a demand for action: to bring back the past

into every present lived by the believer so that by this act of remembering Jesus shall be alive as an active power amidst the community of believers. "The sacrifice offered once for all and unrepeatable, would be continually renewed and become newly present"[62] as the anamnesis of Christ.[63]

I want now to go into a very different cultural area where we find the need for remembering expressed equally strongly although in a different way — that is, in the *Tibetan Book of the Dead*, the *Bardo Thödol*. The ritual performed after the death of the individual, including the reading of the *Bardo Thödol*, is accompanied by the chanting of lamas as a "service for assisting the spirit of the deceased to reach the Western Paradise of Amitabha".[64] Lama Anagarika Govinda, in his introduction to the *Tibetan Book of the Dead*, draws our attention, as a parallel, to the Egyptian *Book of the Dead* and reminds us that "both treatises alike are nothing more than guide-books for the traveller in the realm beyond death".[65] Both are meant to make the spirit of the deceased remember the pitfalls of sangsaric hallu-cinations[66] and to remind him of the "divine principles innate in every human being", like the voidness of *Sunyata*, the Three Bodies — the Tri-Kaya, with the Dharma-Kaya as the highest one — the five wisdoms, etc. To make a digression, we might perhaps find the same archetypal pattern in the Catholic Mass for the deceased: "Requiem aeternam dona eis, Domine, et lux perpetua luceat eis" — "Lord, give them eternal rest, and may the eternal light shine for them." And later: "Deliver the soul of all who believe from the punishments of Hell and of the deep abyss; save them from the lion's jaws that darkness· may not devour them." To return to the *Bardo Thödol*, it serves to recall to the dead the experience of his initiation and the teachings of his guru. The purpose is to restore to the soul the divinity lost at birth — another parallel to the Kabbalistic myth.

This shows a rather paradoxical and negative meaning of memory: by remembering the earthly pleasures and pursuits the dead may be kept prisoner in his low desires. Thus in the next phase, the Chönyid Bardo, the soul may be caught in karmic illusions, resulting from memories and psychic residues of pre-vious existences.[67] In the following phase, the Sidpa Bardo, the last and lowest region of the Bardo, the soul can no longer make use of the previous teachings and is captivated by sexual phantasies, caught by a womb and born again into earthly existence.[68]

This is exactly where the prayers, recitals, and teachings of the lamas present at the funeral chamber are needed. As the Lama Kazi Dawar-Sandrup, the translator of the *Bardo Thödol*, has said: "The forty-nine days of the Bardo symbolize ages either of evolution or of degeneration. Intellects able to grasp the Truth do not fall into the lower conditions of existence."[69] Here we see how the different content and use of memory is decisive: the dead either remembers the karmic illusions or the wisdom teachings; it is either the insistence on our ephemeral existence, or the power of remembering the true concern of the soul.

We find a similar negative assessment of memory in India. The Vedanta speaks of the *vasanas*, the great desires,[70] which, as Vyasa writes in his *Yoga-bhasya* of the fourth century A.D., "have their origin in memory".[71] They are obstacles on the path of liberation, difficult to control and master.

On the other hand a crucial achievement aimed at in Indian philosophy is the recollection of previous births and deaths. In the Anguttara-Nikaya of the Pali Canon, containing part of the sermons of the Buddha, we read of the man who has mastered the yogic method: "Thus he calleth to mind the various appearances and forms of his previous births. This is the first stage of his knowledge; his ignorance (as regards prior births) has vanished, and his knowledge (as regards prior births) hath arisen: darkness hath departed, and light hath arrived...."[72] And the Buddha himself recounts his great revelation under the Bodhi tree: of how he remembered his previous lives, and he gives guidance to his followers how to attain recollection of their lives.

The Buddha attaches great importance to memory. In the Digha-Nikaya, the Book of the Dialogues of Buddha, it is said that even the gods lose their divine condition and fall from their heavens when "their memory is troubled", and "inability to remember *all* of one's former existences is equivalent to metaphysical ignorance.... Because of this 'forgetting' they have a false view of the eternity of the world and of the gods".[73]

In the *Bhagavad Gita* Krishna knows all his births (IV, 5):

> *You and I, Arjuna,*
> *Have lived many lives.*
> *I remember them all:*
> *You do not remember.*

and for Brahmanism as well as Buddhism memory is a divine, precious faculty.

In the Buddha's wake his monks attempted to recollect their earlier lives. Thus it is said of Ananda and other disciples that they "remembered their births", and they are called "rememberers of their births". In the Majjhima-Nikaya, one of the *Further Dialogues*, it is said: "With heart thus steadfast, clarified and purified ... it was thus that I applied my heart to the knowledge which recalled my earlier existences. I called to mind my divers existences in the past, — 'a single birth, then two ... [and so on, to] a hundred thousand births, many an aeon of disintegration of the world, many an aeon of its reintegration."[74] When a Buddhist monk aims at remembering his previous existences, he does so out of disgust with the impermanence of life. Memory provides him with the feeling of immortality.

Whereas to the East life after death and reincarnation are firm tenets, to us Western people they are a great enigma. Jung has devoted a whole chapter in his *Memories* to "Life after Death". There he says that what he can state about it "consists entirely of memories, of images in which I have lived and of thoughts which have buffeted me". Even he, however, is full of doubts. He says: "From the psychological point of view, life in the hereafter world seems to be a logical continuation of the psychic life of old age." But he continues: "We lack concrete proof that anything of us is preserved for eternity. At most we can say that there is some probability that something of our psyche continues beyond physical death. Whether what continues to exist is conscious of itself, we do not know either."[75]

Here seems to be the place to talk of a remarkable theory of memory propounded by Henri Bergson, which could throw light on the hypothesis of survival after death. Bergson has given this theory the name of "souvenir pur", of "pure memory".[76] He states that memory is "a power absolutely independent of matter",[77] in other words that it is a completely "spiritual manifestation" — a phenomenon in which "we can grasp the spirit in its most tangible form". Consequently "any attempt to derive pure memory from an operation of the brain (is) a radical illusion".[78]

Bergson regards the function of the brain, as far as memory is concerned, as fundamentally inhibitory. It prevents us from being swamped by recollections, or rather by recollections which are not "biologically relevant at any particular time",[79] and which "may overflow the usefully associated images".[80] In certain circumstances, such as sleep, this inhibitory brain activity is relaxed, or even suspended, giving rise to — for instance — dreams. In death — and this is the most important point for our discussion — these inhibitory activites come to a complete end. Death frees us from all biological needs, and there is no more place for these previous inhibitions. By this freedom from the inhibitory activity of the brain our whole past is open to our recollection, which most likely takes the form of mental images, derived from our past experiences.[81]

This would mean that records of mental events are laid down in some part of the mind that is not normally accessible during life, and this store of memories could then become manifest after death. In other words: a next world "would be dependent on the memories and desires of the person who experienced it",[82] without any need or possibility of repression. This seems to be very similar to Jung's idea that life after death would consist of memory images. We could put it in parallel with a situation in which Freud's censor no longer functions. This next world could be a world of desires, and the Hindu concept of Kama-Loka, the "world of desire", would fit suitably into such a picture.

If we make use of this Bergsonian theory of memory, works such as those of Charles Williams, in particular *All Hallows' Eve*, begin to make concrete sense. We may also have access to this world usually kept from us until after death by the use of psychedelic drugs. What we usually find as images of the collective unconscious cast up in these drug-induced states may then possess an actual life of their own. So would heaven, purgatory, and hell, and our experiences in life of these and similar states may after all be memories revealed to us by the temporary suspension of the inhibitory function of the brain.

We have only to think of Jung's profound experience in 1944 when a heart attack brought him near to death. He reports this vision in his *Memories*,[83] saying that in it he had reached "the outermost limit". He found himself "high up in space, surveying the whole world". Everything seemed to fall away from him, he felt as if stripped, and at the same time remembered everything he had ever experienced, consisting, as he says, of his own history:[84] "I had everything that I was, and that was everything." He was at the point of entering a temple when he was called back to earth by the appearance of his doctor; profoundly disappointed because he knew that he was at the threshold of complete understanding of, in his own words, "what historical nexus I or my life fitted into. I would know what had been before me, why I had come into being, and where my life was flowing.... I felt sure that I would receive an answer to all these questions...." It took Jung several weeks to get back into earthly life to let go of the memory of a life beyond death, the memory of a knowledge linked to eternity.

Jung's experience is certainly unique in its intensity and beauty, but it is not an isolated incident. I happened to find in *Reader's Digest* the report of a man whom a heart attack had left apparently dead.[85] He was resuscitated 23 minutes after his heart had stopped. Of these 23 minutes he has this to say: "I was part of another world." To put it in his own words, "I felt I've been there and I have come back." Here is his abbreviated report: "When I left my body I also left all sensory human tools behind with which we perceive the world we take to be real. But I found that I now *knew* certain things about my place in our world and my relationship to that other reality.... The last impression I can recall lasted a brief instant. I was moving at high speed towards a net of great luminosity.... The instant I made contact with it, the vibrant luminosity increased to a blinding intensity.... There was no pain.... (It) was like an energy converter transporting me into formlessness, beyond time and space.... This new 'I' was not the I that I knew, but rather a distilled essence of it, yet something vaguely familiar, something I had always known buried under a superstructure of personal fears, hopes, wants and needs. This 'I' was final, unchangeable, indivisible, indestructible pure spirit. While unique and individual as a fingerprint, 'I' was, at the same time, part of some infinite, harmonious and ordered whole. I had been there before. The condition 'I' was in was pervaded by a sense of great stillness and complete quiet. Yet there was also a sense of something momentous about to be revealed, a further change. But there is nothing further to tell except my sudden return to the operating table.... A recurrent nostalgia remains for that other reality.... For the time being I belong to the world and it belongs to me...." I have quoted this report so extensively because it shows so many parallels to Jung's experience and to the idea of the timelessness and spacelessness of the psyche. T.S. Eliot's lines in *Burnt Norton* come to mind:

> *Time present and time past*
> *Are both perhaps present in time future,*
> *And time future contained in time past.*[86]

Both stories, that of Jung's and of an anonymous man, could substantiate Bergson's idea of "pure memory". Both have the feeling of "having been there before", of the recollection of a world and life beyond our earthly world and life. This memory-concept of Bergson's may only be an interesting theory, but there seems to be much in Jung which, to say the least, does not contradict such an idea of pure memory. When Jung talks of the timelessness of "transpsychic reality" carried by the archetypes, when he says that "the life of the psyche requires no space and no time", then a next step may well be to consider the possibility of the continuation of psychic life after death. Here Ovid's words "tempus edax rerum", time is the devourer of all things, take on a new and deeper meaning.

In his *Memories* Jung says that life after death can be only a psychic kind of life and he quotes with approval the dream of a woman of 60 which made it clear that "immediately after death people have to give accounts of the total experience of their lives" — in other words, that their memories were essential at this after-life state. Is it too bold to say that in our dreams we experience, perhaps, a near approximation to what life after death is like?

This may be the place to mention the problems of spooks, haunted houses, and psychometry. A well-known and well-documented phenomenon is that of localised haunting, in which, e.g., a person long dead regularly appears to people sleeping at the place where the ghostly figure once lived. It would seem that such places have retained a memory of past events and people.

Jung himself has experienced and described several such phenomena. In his *Memories* he reports[87] how one night he "awoke to the sound of soft footsteps going around the Tower", and how he also heard laughter, talk, and music. Perhaps even more relevant is his story of the skeleton of the French soldier,[88] which his eldest daughter sensed years before Jung found it while constructing the annex to the Tower. Another story he reported in a contribution to Fanny Moser's book on spooks. He describes a night spent in 1920 in a friend's house in England. There he experienced various phenomena increasing in violence, finally culminating in the appearance of a solid-looking half of a woman's head, staring at him. He learned later that the whole village knew that the house was haunted and that no tenants stayed there for long.[89]

I realize, of course, the highly speculative nature of my observations. There is, however, another phenomenon which may render them more likely: the phenomenon of psychometry. Psychometry is the name given to the apparent power of objects to retain a memory of certain characteristics or experiences of their owners, sometimes of owners long dead.[90] Again, this phenomenon is so well documented that one has to accept it as genuine. Here I might mention Teilhard de Chardin's concept of "cosmogenesis" and of "the within of things", put forward in *The Phenomenon of Man*. According to him, consciousness is not the prerogative of man but exists to constantly diminishing degrees also in animals, plants, and so-called dead matter such as stones. That is to say, that there is "a single energy operating in the world",[91] an idea to which the alchemists' thought[92] of the unity of the universe sounds like a precursor, and which is expressed in the concept of the *unus mundus*. Could it be that we find traces of this belief in stories like that of Orpheus, who could with his music move not only man and beasts but even rocks, or that of Daedalus, who could bring wood to life and make stones walk?

After all, it is already Old Testament belief that all things, animate and inanimate, stand in a relation to God. And two hundred years before Teilhard de Chardin, the Baal Shem, founder of Hasidism, had spoken of the divine sparks, the *nizozot*, which are contained in inanimate matter as well as in animate beings, and have to be redeemed by man.

Martin Buber also, in *Ich und Du*, expresses the idea that the human world of relationship exists not only, even though chiefly, in meeting one's human neighbour; it may extend to animals or trees, and he talks of "a sphere that reaches from stones to stars".[93]

Here we have also to mention the experiments of the great Indian physicist and plant physiologist Sir Jagadis Chandra Bose, which convinced him not only that plants have a definite sensitivity and memory but even that metals, that is inanimate objects, have "some kind of lingering memory".[94] As a consequence of his experiments Bose became convinced that the gulf between so-called inanimate matter and animate life might not be as wide and unbridgeable as science supposed it to be. Even if we have to assume that "dead matter" has only an infintesimally small amount of consciousness, it could nevertheless help explain the phenomenon of psychometry.

Bose's experiments seem to be corroborated by more recent tests with plants, supporting the view that they possess a memory. Such experiments were carried out mainly in the United States by Cleve Backster, and also in Soviet Russia. A Russian experimenter, a prominent member of the Soviet Academy of Sciences, reports that he made "a man molest, even torture a geranium for several days in a row". Among other things "he pinched it, tore it, pricked its leaves with a needle ... and cut its roots. Another man took tender care of the same geranium, watered it ... treated its burns and wounds". When the plant was tested by electrodes connected to very fine instruments, "no sooner did the torturer come near the plant than the recorder of the instrument began to go wild. The plant didn't just get 'nervous', it was afraid, it was horrified.... Hardly had this inquisitor left and the good man taken his place near the plant than the geranium was appeased, its impulses died down, the recorder traced out smooth ... lines on the graph."[95]

Similar results had been achieved before by Backster, whose plants reacted with terror on the approach, or even voice in an adjacent room, of the torturer, but immediately "relaxed" when Backster, who had tended the plant with great care, was near.[96]

From this the experimenters had to conclude that the plant had a memory of what had been done to it by either aggressor or supporter. This leads us back to Bose, who, summing up his experiments, stated: "This vast abode of nature is built in many wings, each with its own portal. The physicist, the chemist and the biologist come in by different doors, each one his own department of knowledge.... Hence has arisen our present division of phenomena into the worlds of inorganic, vegetal and sentient. This philosophical attitude of mind may be denied. We must remember that all inquiries have as their goal the attainment of knowledge in its entirety."[97] Here Bose finds himself on the same line of thought that Jung is on when he talks of the experience of synchronicity. In this experience the duality of matter and psyche is also eliminated, and instead we have a clear indication of the final unity of all being, the *unus mundus*.

I am afraid I have strained the reader's patience and indulgence to breaking point with these speculations, and it seems time to return to more mundane considerations. I would like to accomplish this by considering the second aspect of our theme, that of forgetting. I have mentioned it several times before in passing, but now I want to go into it more specifically. Strangely enough, forgetting is a much more complex function than remembering, showing many and often contradictory, aspects.

One of the aspects of forgetting that is most different is that, although you can train your memory, develop a mnemotechnique, it is next to impossible to develop a technique of forgetting. Matthew Arnold expresses this in his lines:

> *And we forget because we must*
> *And not because we will*[97a]

Themistocles, the great Athenian statesman of the fifth century B.C., had stated that he "preferred the science of forgetting to that of remembering".[98] And Shereshevskii, the memory prodigy whom I mentioned at the beginning, made desperate but futile attempts to forget what he had learned by writing it down and then burning the paper. Actually in time he discovered how to forget by the use of willpower.[99]

Forgetting has always been a problem for psychologists. I need only mention the great importance that Freud and psychoanalysis gave it, as I pointed out at the beginning of my essay. As early as 1898, Freud published a paper on "The Psychical Mechanism of Forgetting", six years before *The Psychopathology of Everyday Life* (1904). There the first chapter has the title "The Forgetting of Proper Names", and three more chapters deal with the same problem. It may not be necessary to go further into the well-known mechanism of repression.

Equally, I want to mention only briefly Jung's interest in the matter in addition to what I have said in the beginning. Following the theories Janet published in 1893 in *The Mental State of Hystericals*, Jung discusses hysterical forgetfulness in his doctoral dissertation, and we find frequent references to amnesia in his early psychiatric writings. In the *Studies in Word Association* we find a paper on "Experimental Observations of the Faculty of Memory", and here he mentions Freud's work on the subject with appreciation, accepting Freud's idea that forgetting has to be equated with repression.[100] He explains amnestic blockages and faulty reproductions of reaction words as due to repressed complexes.[101] I might also mention the basic essay "On Psychic Energy" of 1928 or the "Review of the Complex Theory" of 1934.[102]

After having given their due to the pioneers of a dynamic theory of forgetting, I would like to go back in history in the same way as I did when discussing the subject of memory. Here again we find ourselves in the company of the Greeks. As I have said, Mnemosyne, Memory, and Lesmosyne or Lethe, Forgetting, were twin concepts to the ancient Greeks. To them forgetting had various functions.

There is first of all the negative side. In the dialogue *Gorgias*

Plato compares the soul of the foolish and uninitiated to a sieve, "because it is perforated and through lack of belief and forgetfulness unable to hold anything".[103] I have mentioned the *Phaedrus*, where Plato describes the fate of the soul which, in her negative state, is "burdened with a load of forgetfulness and, not following a God, has to live in a perishable body". As George Meredith wrote almost two and a half millenniums later in his novelette *Modern Love*[103a]:

> *And if I drink oblivion of a day,*
> *So shorten I the stature of my soul.*

Another version of the fate of the soul we find in Plato's *Republic*, where he describes, right at the end, how the souls, after having "chosen their lives in the order of their lots" and after having passed the three Moirai, goddesses of fate, journey to the "Plain of Oblivion", where they camp by the "River of Forgetfulness whose waters no vessel can contain". There they are "all required to drink a measure of the water, and those who were not saved by their good sense drink more than the measure, and each one as he drank forgot all things".[104]

Whereas in Plato's myth all souls to be reborn have to drink from Lethe, the Orphic mysteries taught their initiates to avoid the waters of Lethe altogether and instead to drink only of the nearby waters of Mnemosyne.[105]

Plato's version in the *Republic* represents an initiatory experience: the initiate has to drink from Lethe in order to obtain his new life on earth. Thus Lethe, the water of the underworld, is at the same time the water of life, and only after drinking does the will to exist begin to assert itself. Virgil says it in the *Aeneid*: "In corpora velle reverti", "they begin to wish to be born again".[196]

The initiatory significance of Lethe, or Lesmosyne, is apparent in the incubation rituals at Lebadeia, where the oracles of Trophonios, a half-brother of Asklepios, were given.[107] The suppliant had to undergo a *katabasis* into the cave of Trophonios after having drunk from the waters of Lethe, which would help him forget his past, and from the waters of Mnemosyne, which would enable him to remember all he was going to see and hear

down in the cave. There an invisible voice revealed the future
to him, but when the voice had finished he lost all sense and
understanding. On his return he was set on the so-called "Chair
of Memory" and asked to repeat what he had experienced.
This gave him the required oracle which Trophonios, in the
shape of a serpent, had announced to him in the cave, and which
was now interpreted by the priests. I shall have to say more
later on about this ritual forgetting as pre-condition for renewal.
The double aspect of Lethe and Mnemosyne is also mentioned in
Dante's *Purgatorio* (Canto 28), where they are significantly one
river dividing into two arms: Lethe, taking away the memory of
all sins, and Mnemosyne, called by Dante Eunoe, good memory,
which restores the memory of all good deeds.

Lethe, taking away the memory of sins, leads us over to the
soothing function of forgetting. This played an important role in
ancient thought. Aeschylus lets accursed Orestes say, "Oh goddess of forgetting, Lethe, how wise you are to whom pray the
poor", and Virgil talks of "the waters that quench man's trouble,
the deep draught of oblivion".[108] Shakespeare's words that he
lets Macbeth speak echo Orestes' words:

> *Canst thou not minister to a mind diseas'd,*
> *Pluck from the memory a rooted sorrow,*
> *Race out the written troubles of the brain,*
> *And with some sweet oblivious antidote*
> *Cleanse the stuff'd bosom of that perilous stuff*
> *Which weighs upon the heart?*

With this we may leave the ancients and go over to a very
different kind of civilisation, to the world of shamanism. Here we
meet with forgetting mostly as a *rite de passage*.[109] To put it
into a nutshell: before the novice, aiming at the full stature of the
shaman, can achieve his goal, he has to forget, or to act as if he
had forgotten his ordinary behaviour and must learn everything
anew.[110] In order to participate in a higher and more potent
life, the novice has to forget his previous way of life.

Occasionally an individual destined to become a shaman will
suddenly lose consciousness,[111] become absent minded or

dreamy, or forget his usual behaviour.[112] Spencer and Gillen, in *The Native Tribes of Central Australia*, report the case of a famous magician who, when he was made into a medicine man, underwent the psychic experience of symbolic disembowelling by a very old doctor, who then provided him with a complete set of new internal parts. When he returned to life, he had no idea where he was, having "completely forgotten who he was and all about his past life". On awakening, the old doctor told the novice "No, you are not lost; I killed you a long time ago."[113] Here death, complete amnesia, is the bridge into a new mode of life, a typical *rite de passage*, of forgetting the old and receiving the new. The sequence is always the same: suffering, death, resurrection, or as we could also say: suffering, forgetting, remembering.

Often the instruction of the shaman happens in dreams when ego-consciousness is at its lowest — as it were, forgotten. "It is in dreams that the pure sacred life is entered and direct relations with the gods, spirits, and ancestral souls are re-established. It is always in dreams that historical time is abolished and the mythical time regained."[114] Here we find ourselves again in the world of the archetypes, but in contradistinction to the kind of archetypal dream we know and have to deal with, the shaman's dreaming represents complete oblivion of previous empirical existence. Physical ordeals, which are a frequent part of initiation, are meant to let the novice forget what we would call his ego; suffering and pain open him up to the influx of the unconscious images, of the primordial situation of the human condition before the fall.[115]

I now want to leave the subject of shamanism in order to consider the problem of forgetting as we meet it in Indian philosophy. I have mentioned before some of the negative connotations of forgetting, as, e.g., in the forgetting of previous births and deaths. Now, however, I should like to concentrate on the positive side, where we find the highest stage of forgetting, which I might call the transcendental stage, leading to an experience of the divine, of the numinous transcendental.

Basically Indian philosophy rests on the idea of abstracting from all manifestations of life outward and inward, to forgo and forget all "sense-impressions and feelings, thoughts and aspirations", as the condition for sinking "into the pure silent spirit"[116] which is the force behind the unfolding of our life. Sarvepalli Radhakrishnan, the great Indian philosopher and statesman, has this to say: "It is a condition of consciousness in which feelings are fused, ideas melt into one another, boundaries broken and ordinary distinctions transcended. Past and present fade away in a sense of timeless being.... We forget the sense of the outward world in our communion with the grandeur beyond."[117] These words are applicable as much to mystic experience in general as to the Indian experience in particular. Forgetting the sense of the outward world, stilling the desires of the heart, overcoming the *kleshas*, the hindrances on the way to liberation, is a constant theme of Indian philosophy, be it in the Vedas or Upanishads, in the Mahabharata or in the Buddha's teachings.

The Maitri-Upanishad speaks of the great forgetting as "making the mind motionless", as "mindlessness":

By making mind all motionless,
From sloth and from distraction freed,
When unto mindlessness one comes,
Then that is the supreme estate.[118]

The Mundaka Upanishad speaks of those "who are perfected selves, from passion free, tranquil.... So the knower, being liberated from name and form, goes unto the Heavenly Person, higher than the high".[119] In the Bhagavad Gita we read of the man who "puts away all the desires of his mind",[120] "without any sense of mineness or egotism — he attains to peace".[121] Another passage talks of the "man whose attachments are sundered ... who is dissolved entirely", meaning that his actions do not bind him any longer to cosmic existence; that, forgetting the ties of the world, he has become liberated. The Mahabharata, of which the Gita is the most important section, speaks of the man "said to be truly learned and truly possessed of wisdom" as the one "who abandons every act ... who is completely dissociated from all wordly surroundings, and who has renounced everything that appertains to the world".[122] What greater forgetting could there be than this abandoning, forgetting the world around oneself, for the purpose of liberation?

This is, of course, the centre of the Buddha's teaching as well. The Dhammapada, the Path of Virtue, is full of exhortations to forget the desires of this world, as when it says: "Give up what is before, give up what is behind, give up what is in the middle, passing to the farther shore of existence. When your mind is wholly freed you will not again return to birth and old age."[123] The Buddha admonishes one of his disciples, saying: "The saint, O Vaccha, who has been released from what is styled consciousness, is deep, immeasurable, unfathomable, like the mighty ocean."[124] One of the most beautiful of the Buddha's utterances we find in the Udana, part of the Pali Canon: "Monks, there exists that condition wherein is neither earth nor water nor fire nor air: wherein is neither the sphere of infinite space nor of infinite consciousness nor of nothingness nor of neitherconsciousness-nor-unconsciousness; where there is neither this world nor a world beyond nor both together nor moon-and-sun. Thence, monks, I declare is no coming to birth; thither is no going from life; therein is no duration; thence is no falling; there is no arising. It is not something fixed, it moves not on, it is not based on anything. That indeed is the end of ill."[125]

Only in passing do I want to mention the concept of *Sunyata*, the Great Void, in the teaching of the Mahayana, the Great Vehicle, as developed by Nagarjuna.[126] This concept of the void or emptiness, which forms the basis of Zen Buddhism, expresses all the forms of non-attachment, of forgetting egoconsciousness, which we have found in our mentioned examples. And in China Yen Hui tells his master Confucius: "I cast aside my limbs, discard my intelligence, detach from both body and mind, and become one with the Great Universal (Tao). This is called sitting down and forgetting everything".[127]

Right into modern times, I could adduce example after example of this particular attitude, showing the specific Indian mode of forgetfulness. We find many parallels in Western or Islamic mysticism but with a characteristic difference: whereas in Indian thought forgetting is the path to liberation from the illusion of maya, in Western and Islamic mysticism forgetfulness of this world and of ego-consciousness is the way towards fusion with the Godhead. The forgetting of the ego produces a particular dilemma to which I shall return later.

If I now want to concern myself with the mystics of the Middle Ages, it may be important to remember that to Jung the *consensus omnium* was a strong and acceptable factor in proving the psychic reality of an experience. In this connection it is significant that we find the same archetypal pattern of the insistence on egolessness, expressed in the forgetting of the ego's concern with this world, not only in the Far East but also in our Western culture, among the great mystics of Germany, England, Spain, or Italy, or of Jewish Hasidism, and in the near East among the devotees of Islam.

It is next to impossible to make a selection among these people who dedicated their lives to the pursuit of the Divine. I collected dozens of illustrations, but I shall have to omit most of them and use the example of the few for clarification of my thesis. Before going into any details I would like to quote Jung. In his essay "Concerning Rebirth" he speaks of natural transformation or individuation as demanding a death or a rebirth.[128] And in "A Study in the Process of Individuation" he talks of "letting go" as "the *sine qua non* of all forms of higher spiritual development, whether we call it meditation, contemplation, yoga, or spiritual exercises.... Relinquishment of the ego is not an act of the will and not a result arbitrarily produced; it is an event, an occurrence, whose inner, compelling logic can be disguised only by wilful self-deception. In this case and at this moment the ability to 'let go' is of decisive importance. But since everything passes, the moment may come when the relinquished ego must be reinstated in its functions."[129] These words of Jung seem to allow for the possibility of at least temporarily "relinquishing" the ego, of temporary egolessness.

It is with this "letting go" that mystics in general are concerned. I realize that the accumulation of examples may be oppressive, but I cannot see any other way to convey the experience of these mystics. The tradition is old and long. In the first century A.D., Philo Judaeus speaks of "the influence of divine inspiration" through which he has "known neither the place in which I was,

nor those who were present, nor myself",[130] and the Neoplatonist Plotinus talks two centuries later of the "other kind of
perception, a going out of oneself and becoming simple, a giving
oneself away" as the precondition for "seeing the eternal being in
the inner sanctuary",[131] or, as we might say: forgetting the ego
in favour of the self.

Neoplatonism greatly influenced Dionysius the Areopagite, the
pseudonymous mystical theologian of the fourth or fifth century.
His idea that to live is to be united with God is the basic
ingredient of the mystical thought of the Middle Ages and the
sixteenth century. His influence is also felt particularly in the
Eastern Church, in the mystical movement of Hesychasm, of the
Prayer of the Heart, which I can only mention in passing.

One of the earliest German mystics, Mechthild von Magdeburg, living in the thirteenth century, exclaims, "Du sollst
minnen das Nicht, du sollst fliehen das Icht": "Thou shall woo
the nothingness, thou shall flee the ego," expressing again the
need for egolessness, for forgetting, as the way towards the *unio
mystica*,[132] and later, in the same century or the beginning of
the next, Meister Eckhardt demands that man become freed of
himself and of all things, for "Where the creative man ends, there
God begins".[133] Only by forgetting oneself can one approach
God. In the fourteenth century the unknown author of the
Theologia Deutsch, the "German Theology", quotes Dionysius
the Areopagite: "In order to see God's secret, you have to
abandon senses and sensuality; you should concentrate on letting
go of yourself, forgetting all the fore-named things".[134] The
same century hears Johannes Tauler, the Doctor Illuminatus,
preach: "Dear Child, drown into the divine ground, into your
nothingness." To him the *deus absconditus*, "the divine darkness
which is of unspeakable clarity",[135] is the aim of contemplation: "Towards it carry your own abysmal darkness and let the
abyss of the divine darkness illuminate you." Here he is near St.
Augustine's *abditum mentis*, the hiddenness of the soul, which is
nearest to God. A century later Thomas à Kempis, in the *Imitatio
Christi*, talks of the necessity "to die to oneself" if one wants to live
for God. Jacob Böhme, almost 150 years later, experiences the
"*Ungrund*, the nothingness, which goes still deeper than God", as

the "primal preexistential freedom"[136] which can be met only by man's utter nakedness and nothingness, by giving himself up utterly and completely, by forgetting all but the craving for this *Ungrund*, this nothingness.

Over two centuries earlier an anonymous English monk in his *Cloud of the Unknowing* held forth[137] that the necessary preliminary of any true communion with the spirit is to be freed from all distractions of memory, that all memories and thoughts have to be "trodden down under the cloud of forgetting" until "nothing lives in the working mind but a naked intent stretching to God".[138] The cloud of unknowing is the "divine darkness, [139] the cloud of ignorance, dark with excess of light". In a telling phrase he declaims: "'and if ever thou shall come through this cloud ... right so put a cloud of forgetting beneath thee.... Thou art well further from Him when thou hast no cloud of forgetting betwixt thee and all the creatures that ever been made [for] thou shalt in this work forget both thyself and also thy deeds for God."[140]

I could continue with quotations until one felt utterly drowned. I shall risk just two more, for no discussion of the subject could omit mentioning St. Teresa of Avila and St. John of the Cross. St. Teresa comes strongly down on memory: memory and imagination "when they are left alone, it is marvellous to see what havoc they make, and how they try to throw everything into disorder.... I am wearied by these disorderly faculties and I loathe them.... Often I pray God to rid me of them".[141] At another place[142] we read: "I forget everything in my longing to see God; and this abandonment and loneliness seems better than all the company in the world." Complete forgetting is needed: all natural functions of the psyche, be they seeing or hearing or understanding, have to be suspended for the communion with God. The ego has to "die to the world, so that the self, the spirit, can be freed for the dawning of the inner light". Jacob Böhme calls out "Not I, the I that I am, know these things; but God knows them in me", paraphrasing the words "Yet not I, but Christ liveth in me" (Gal. 2:20).

Equally St. John of the Cross, the great pupil and friend of St. Teresa, speaks of the withdrawal and detachment from all things needed for approaching the Deity. In a stanza of the "Ascent of Mount Carmel" he sings:

> With his gentle hand he wounded my neck
> And caused all my senses to be suspended.
> I remained, lost in oblivion; my face I reclined on the Beloved
> All ceased and I abandoned myself,
> Leaving my cares forgotten among the lilies.[143]

I shall make just one more digression, this time again into Islam and Judaism. Islam has developed its specific brand of mysticism in Sufism. Listen to Farid ud-din Attar, a Sufi of the twelfth century: "Whose heart is lost in the ocean of infinity is lost there for ever and remains in peace. Fold the mantle of nothingness around yourself and drink of the cup of annihilation. I am wiped out, I have disappeared; nothing of myself remains."[144] And to end with mysticism, two short stories of two Zaddiks, the masters of Hasidism.

The first one is told of Rabbi Elimelekh of Lizhensk, one of the earliest Hasidim, who lived in the eighteenth century: "When Rabbi Elimelekh said the Prayer of Sanctification on the Sabbath, he occasionally took out his watch and looked at it. For in that hour, his soul threatened to dissolve in bliss, and so he looked at his watch in order to steady himself in Time and the world."[145] The other one is of Rabbi Shelomo of Karlin, also of the eighteenth century: "Someone asked Rabbi Shelomo of Karlin to promise to visit him the next day. "How can you ask me to make such a promise?" said the Zaddik. "This evening I must pray and recite 'Hear, O Israel'. While I say these words, my soul goes to the utmost rim of life. And when it is day, the great Morning Prayer is apacing through all worlds, and finally, when I fall on my face, my soul leans over the rim of life. Perhaps I shall not die this time either, but how can I now promise to do something at a time after the prayer?"[146] One could go on and on, and I have omitted all references to modern forms of mysticism, but I think even the few passages I quoted show one thing convincingly: that the great forgetting, the abandonment, the letting go, the "sich entäussern", the surrender of the ego to the self, is at the heart of all mystical experience, its hallmark. It has been poignantly expressed by D.H. Lawrence: "Are you willing to be made nothing? dipped into oblivion? If not, you will never really change."[146a] And a year before his death, William Blake wrote into the autograph album of a friend: "William Blake, born 28 November 1757 in London and has died several times since."[147]

But the mystical experience confronts us with a difficult quandary: how is it possible for the devotee to remember his experiences when his ego-consciousness is suspended, when he is, as for instance the idea of Sunyata, the Great Void, describes it, in a state of egolessness. This is a problem which has attracted and vexed Jung frequently. He had some extensive correspondence about this perplexing question with many of his friends and pupils. As late as 1958 Jung wrote that the *satori* experience would not be possible without a conscious ego.[148]

One could even say that it is one idea that Jung puts constantly forward: it is that without ego-consciousness we could not experience at all, and that we certainly could not remember anything in a state of egolessness. He put it succinctly in a letter to V. Subrahamanya Iyer, the guru of the Maharajah of Mysore, of August 1938,[149] where he says: "If you eradicate the ego completely, there is nobody left that could consciously experience ... If you abolish the ego altogether, then you create unconsciousness.' And in another letter he repeats much later, in December 1958,[150] that without ego there cannot be memory, and that the assumption of an imageless state is an uncritical and unpsychological statement.

Jung seems to express a slightly less negative attitude in his commentary to a seminar given by the German professor of Sanscrit, Wilhelm Hauer on Kundalini Yoga in Zürich in 1932. There he says[151] that the para-aspect of Kundalini Yoga is for us a purely theoretical abstraction, whereas for Indian thought such hypostasized abstractions are much more concrete and substantial because to the Indian the Brahman, the Purusha, represents *the* undoubted fact. To us, so he says, they are the last results of an extremely bold speculation. This seems to leave the question somewhat more open and the answer more relative. But on the whole Jung's point of view contrasts strongly with the Indian point of view that there exists an egoless consciousness of the Atman, the ultimate Reality. To the Western mind this is a metaphysical assertion, and, therefore, unprovable.

Jung very rightly defends here the Western epistemological approach. On the other hand, we have a statement like that of William James in *The Varieties of Religious Experience*, where he says: "The overcoming of all the usual barriers between the individual and the Absolute is the great mystic achievement. In mystic states we both become one with the Absolute and we become aware of our oneness."[152] And a modern twentieth-century Indian thinker — and one of the greatest — Sri Aurobindo, still maintains: "Man's task on earth is to achieve identity with the Absolute by passing beyond the realm of the mental" — we would say psychic — "through a supra-mental stage; the mental level does not constitute the limit of man's progress because it does not constitute the limit of his fundamental nature."[153]

I must admit that I have often been vexed by this problem. Much as I am inclined to accept Jung's authority on such a question, I cannot help experiencing a profound sympathy with the Indian point of view, and I cannot but feel that the thinkers of Buddhism or of the Vedanta have something to say about Reality with a capital R. And has not Jung himself opened it up again when, in his brilliant introduction to *Psychology and Alchemy*, he says: "When I say as a psychologist that God is an archetype, I mean by that the 'type' in the psyche. The word 'type' is, as we know, derived from *typos*, 'blow' or 'imprint'; thus" — and here come the decisive words — "thus an archetype presupposes an imprinter.... We simply do not know the ultimate derivation of the archetype any more than we know the origin of the psyche."[154] Here it seems to me he defines two different worlds, that of empirical research and that of the unknowable — but by no means fantastic — area beyond it. Could it be that the empiricist in Jung and the visionary, the physician and the meta-physician, lived side by side in a sometimes uneasy relationship, and that it was only Jung's scientific conscience that made him so critical of a world to which he had undoubtedly access? However, that may be, for myself I have to leave the answer open.[155]

Perhaps a letter which Jung wrote in 1960,[156] very near the end of his life, can help us one step further: in his letter he discusses the problem of postmortal phenomena, and the question of an out-of-time state. He states that crossing the borderline between being-in-time and being-out-of-time is extremely difficult. This, however, he continues, does not prevent the two times from existing in a parallel manner and that it is even possible that we "may simultaneously exist in both worlds, and occasionally we do have intimations of a twofold existence". Could it be that the parallel existence is also one in which we need a conscious ego for our ordinary experience and also another one in which this conscious ego is suspended and another consciousness, that of a deeper self, takes over? Could it not be that we have experiences which become conscious and formulated only after awakening from the state of union but which have nevertheless been truly experienced, that we have been immersed into timelessness? This leaves the possibility open that genuine mystics have found their own way to cross this border, that they have not only an intuition of the two worlds but have actually experienced them. The Zen Master Kenshin says: "there is something in you which is above birth-and-death and which is neither drowned in water nor burned by fire. I myself have gained an insight into this *samadhi* and know what I am telling you. Those who are reluctant to give up their lives and embrace death are not true warriors."[157]

It may be that we all cross this difficult frontier between being-in-time and being-out-of-time in death. It may be that death is not only the final forgetting but also the beginning of ultimate memory.

In the Katha Upanishad we read:[158]

> Higher than the senses are the objects of sense.
> Higher than the objects of sense is the mind;
> And higher than the mind is the intellect.
> Higher than the intellect is the Great Self.
> Higher than the Great Self is the Unmanifest.
> Higher than the Unmanifest is the Person.
> Higher than the Person there is nothing at all.
> That is the goal. That is the highest course.

REFERENCES

1 "We Jews are a community based on memory. A common memory has kept us together and enabled us to survive." Martin Buber, *Israel and the World* (New York, 1948), p.146

2 F.C. Bartlett, *Remembering: A Study in Experimental and Social Psychology* (Cambridge, 1932)

3 Standard Edn., Vol.6; London, 1960

4 Quoted in Erwin Stengel, "Psychogenic Loss of Memory", in C.W.M. Whitty and O.L. Zangwill, eds., *Amnesia* (London, 1966)

5 "On Simulated Insanity", CW 1, par. 319. (CW = Collected Works of C.G. Jung, New York/Princeton and London.)

6 In CW 1.

7 In CW 2.

8 CW 18, par. 18

9 Ibid., par. 77

10 Ibid., fig. 4

11 CW 1, par. 138

12 The poet W.B. Yeats writes (*Mythologies*, New York, 1959, p.345): "Before the mind's eye, whether in sleep or waking, came images one was to discover presently in some book one had never read, and after looking in vain for explanation to the current theory of forgotten personal memory, I came to believe in a Great Memory passing on from generation to generation."

13 Karl Kerényi, "Hermes der Seelenführer," *Eranos-Jahrbuch 1942* (Zürich, 1943), p.41

14 Kerényi, *The Gods of the Greeks,* tr. N. Cameron (London and New York, 1951), p.103

15 Ibid.

16 Quoted in Frances A. Yates, *The Art of Memory* (Harmondsworth, 1969), p.59

17 Ibid., pp.17-19

18 Luria, A.R. "Memory and the Structure of Mental Processes," *Problems of Psychology*, No. 1 (London, 1960), p.87

19 Ibid., pp.82f.

20 Wolfgang Pauli, "The Influence of Archetypal Ideas on the Scientific Theories of Kepler," tr. p. Silz, in *The Interpretation of Nature and the Psyche* (London and New York, 1955).

21 Yates, p.366

22 Ibid., p.68

23 *Confessions*, tr. F.J. Sheed (London and New York, 1951), Vol. 8, pp.172, 174

24 Yates, p.62

25 "Lethe" had originally the meaning of "being hidden" (cf. Kerényi, "Mnemosyne-Lesmosyne", in *Spring* 1977, Zürich, p.121), hence being hidden from knowledge, conveying the idea of forgetting. Martin Heidegger

in (*Being and Time*, 1962, pp.56f., and in *An Introduction to Metaphysics*,
1959, pp.86, 159) has interpreted the Greek word for "truth", *aletheia*, as
being formed as the negative to *lethaia*, that is, as *a-letheia*, thus understanding "truth" as what is unconcealed, discovered (remembered!). Heidegger's etymology has, however, been severely criticised by Paul Fried-
länder in his *Plato*, Vol.1 (Princeton and London, 2nd edn., 1969),
pp.225f.

26 J.O. Plassman, tr., *Orpheus, altgriechische Mysteriengesänge* (Jena, 1928),
p.100. English tr. by kindness of Dr. David Phillips.

27 *Philebus*, 35 b, tr. R. Hackforth. (This and other quotations of Plato are
from the Bollingen *Collected Dialogues*, ed. Edith Hamilton and Hunting-
ton Cairns, New York, 1961.) Cf. Plotinus: The soul "makes its memories
the starting point of a new vision of essential being" (quoted from Kathleen
Raine, "The Inner Journey of the Poet", in *Harvest*, No.22, London, 1976,
p.74.)

28 *Phaedrus*, 248 c/d, tr. R. Hackfroth.

29 Arnold Hauser, *The Social History of Art*, Vol.2 (London, 1962), p.39

30 Quoted in Philip Rawson, "Western Visions of Unity", in Ajit Mookerjee,
Yoga Art (London, 1975), p.172

31 Jung, "On the Nature of the Psyche", CW 8, par. 351.

32 Quoted in Angelo S. Rappoport, *The Folklore of the Jews* (London, 1937),
p.92

33 Martin Buber, *Tales of the Hasidim: Early Masters* (New York, 1947), p.96

34 Paul Deussen, *Sechzig Upanishad's des Veda* (Leipzig, 1921), p.610

35 Ibid., p.182

36 Ibid., p.249

37 Mircea Eliade, *Yoga: Immortality and Freedom* (New York, 1958), p.314

38 M.R. James, ed., *The Apocryphal New Testament* (Oxford, 1924), pp.411ff

39 CW 11, par. 814

40 Quoted in Rawson, p.193

41 "On Synchronicity", CW 8, par. 974

42 *Memories, Dreams, Reflections by C.G. Jung*, recorded and edited by
Aniela Jaffé (New York and London, 1963), pp.254f./283. (Double page
refs. pertain to the New York and London paperback edns. respectively.)

43 Quoted in William James, *The Varieties of Religious Experience* (New York
and London, 1929), p.374

44 Ibid., p.375

45 Pp.254ff./283

46 Cf. Dante, *Paradiso*, XVII, 17f.: "... il punto / a cui tutti li tempi son
presenti" (the Point to which all times are present); also XXIX, 12: "... là
've s'appunta ogni *ubi* e ogne *quando*" (here where every *where* and *when*
is centred). (Tr. C.S. Singleton, Princeton, 1975, mod.) Cf. also Jung, "The
Psychology of the Transference", CW 16, par. 468, n.8: "... the 'timeless'
quality of the unconscious, where conscious succession becomes simultan-
eity", and *Memories*, pp.295f./326f. Equally to the disciple of Zen "all

action occurs in an infinite present. ... All events occur simultaneously" Robert E. Ornstein, *The Psychology of Consciousness*, London, 1975, p.107).

47 Ajit Mookerjee, p.44 and pl.7.

48 Heinrich Zimmer, *Myths and Symbols in Indian Art and Civilization* (New York, 1946), p.149

48a Rainer Maria Rilke, *Duino Elegies* tr. J.B. Leishmann and Stephen Spender, (London, 1939).

48b Goethe, *Lyrische und Epische Dichtungen*, Bd 1, Leipzig, 1923, p. 192

49 CW 11, par.640

50 Quoted in M. Esther Harding, *Psychic Energy: Its Source and Its Transformation*, 2nd edn. (New York, 1963), p.210

51 *Remembrance of Things Past: Swann's Way*, tr. C.K. Scott Moncrieff (London, 1955), p.61

52 Pp.158f./182f.

53 Ibid., p.161/184

54 Ibid., pp.202f./228f.

55 Gerhard Adler, *The Living Symbol* (New York and London, 1961), p.98

56 Ibid., p.166

57 Tr. Wong Moulam (London, 1944), p.23 and n.

58 "Flying Saucers: A Modern Myth of Things Seen in the Skies", CW 10, par. 600

59 Ibid., par. 622

60 Robert Graves, *The Greek Myths* (Harmondsworth, 1955), Vol.2, p.113, and C.A. Meier, *Ancient Incubation and Modern Psychotherapy*, tr. M. Curtis (Evanston, 1967), p.6

61 "The State of Psychotherapy Today", CW 10, par. 361

62 A.G. Herbert, "Memory, Memorial, Remember, Remembrance", in Alan Richardson, ed., *A Theological Word Book of the Bible* (London, 1950).

63 Regarding the problem of God's memory, the Protestant theologian Paul Tillich has made an interesting contribution. In his *Systematic Theology* (Vol.3, Chicago, 1963, London, 1964, p.400) he suggests that man is immortal in the sense that his earthly life possesses an eternal presence within God's eternal memory. This divine memory is selective, remembering only the good and forgetting the bad. He says: "... the negative side is not an object of eternal memory in the sense of living retention. Neither is it forgotten, for forgetting pre-supposes at least a moment of remembering. The negative is not remembered at all. It is acknowledged for what it is — non-being...." Quoted from John H. Hick, *Death and Eternal Life* (New York 1976), p.215

64 W.Y. Evans-Wentz, ed., *The Tibetan Book of the Dead* (London, 1957), p.20

65 Ibid., p.22

66 Ibid., p.17

67 Jung, "Psychological Commentary on 'The Tibetan Book of the Dead,'" CW 11, par. 845

68 Ibid., par. 842

69 Evans-Wentz, introduction, p.44

70 Sarvepalli Radhakrishnan and Charles A. Moore, eds., *A Source Book in Indian Philosophy* (Princeton, 1957), p.561

71 Eliade, *Yoga*, p.42

72 Evans-Wentz, p.41

73 Eliade, p.183

74 Ibid., p.182

75 *Memories*, pp.299/330, 320/351, 322/354

76 Bergson, *Matter and Memory* (London, 1911), pp.71ff., 170, and passim

77 Ibid., p.81

78 Ibid., p.326

79 Henry Habberley Price, "Survival and the Idea of Another World", in J.R. Smythies, ed., *Brain and Mind* (London, 1965), p.32

80 Bergson, p.97

81 Price, p.32

82 Ibid., p.17. Related to this idea seems the concept of the Catholic theologian Karl Rahner, in *On the Theology of Death* (London and New York, 1965), p.20, quoted from Hick, *Death and Eternal Life*, p.228: "In death the soul becomes *nicht akosmisch, sondern allkosmisch* — not acosmic, but pancosmic." At death the soul is released from the limitations of a particular bit of the world, namely of the human body, and becomes instead related to the world as a whole.

83 Pp.289ff./320ff.

84 Ibid., p.291/322

85 "I Died at 10.52", *Reader's Digest*, February, 1975, pp.103ff. (by permission)

86 T.S. Eliot, Burnt Norton, London: Faber and Faber, 1969 (by permission).

87 Pp.229ff./256f.

88 Ibid., pp.231f./258f.

89 Contribution to Fanny Moser, *Spuk: Irrglaube oder Wahrglaube?* (Baden bei Zürich, 1950); in CW 18, pars. 764ff.

90 Cf. Thomas Aquinas, *Exp. Phys.* IV, lect. 1, n.412: "Place has a certain power of conserving that which is located in place. And because of this, that which is located in place tends toward its own place by a desire for its own conservation." Quoted from C.S. Singleton, Commentary to Dante's *Purgatorio* (Princeton, 1973), pp.418f. Cf. also Jung, "The Language of Dreams", CW 18, par. 480: "There are numerous well authenticated stories of a clock that stopped at the moment of its owner's death, like Frederick the Great's pendulum clock at Sans Souci; of a mirror that broke, or a boiling coffeepot that exploded, just before or during a crisis ..."

91 Pierre Teilhard de Chardin, *The Phenomenon of Man* (London, 1965), p.69

92 Cf. Jung, *Aion*, CW 9, ii, par. 367: "... alchemy began to develop its conception of Mercurius as the partly material, partly immaterial spirit that penetrates and sustains all things, from stones and metals to the highest

living organisms." Also par. 389: "... the metals grow from Gayomart's blood."

93 Buber, *Ich und Du* (Cologne, 1966), p.149. (This passage does not appear in the earlier English translation *I and Thou*.) Cf. also Dante, *Paradiso*, I, 109-117. Singleton, in his commentary to the passage, says on "tutte nature" (p.25): "All created things, animate and inanimate, stones and flames, as well as animals, men, and angels, are included in this perception."

94 Peter Tompkins and Christopher Bird, *The Secret Life of Plants* (Harmondsworth, 1975), p.85

95 Ibid., pp.73f.

96 Lyall Watson, *Supernature*, (London, 1974), pp.247f.

97 Tompkins and Bird, pp.91f.

97a Matthew Arnold, "Absence", *Poetical Works*, London, 1969, p.183

98 Yates, *The Art of Memory*, p.32

99 Nigel Calder, *The Mind of Man* (London, 1970), p.116

100 "Experimental Observations on the Faculty of Memory," CW 2, par. 640

101 Ibid., par. 657

102 Both essays in CW 8

103 *Gorgias*, 493 c, tr. W.D. Woodhead

103a George Meredith, *Poems*, vol.I, p.14, Westminster, 1902. Modern Love, xii

104 Plato. *Republic*, 621 b/c, tr. P. Shorey

105 Kerényi, *The Gods of the Greeks*, pp.246f.

106 *Aeneid*, Book VI, 751

107 Robert Graves, Vol.1, pp.179f.; Meier, p.97

108 *Aeneid*, Book VI, 715

109 Gerardus van der Leeuw, *Religion in Essence and Manifestation* tr. J.E. Turner (London, 1938), p.192; Adler, *The Living Symbol*, p.178

110 van der Leeuw, p.197

111 Eliade, *Shamanism: Archaic Techniques of Ecstasy* (New York, 1964), p.16

112 Ibid., p.19

113 Ibid., pp.47f.

114 Ibid., p.103

115 Ibid., p.493

116 Radhakrishnan and Moore, p.632

117 Ibid., pp.617f.

118 Ibid., p.96

119 Ibid., p.55

120 Ibid., p.110

121 Ibid., p.112

122 Ibid., p.168

123 Ibid., p.319

124 Ibid., p.292

125 Ibid., pp.327f.

126 Heinrich Zimmer, *Philosophies of India*, (New York, 1951), pp.509f.

127 Wing-tsit Chan, *A Source Book in Chinese Philosophy* (Princeton, 1973), p.201

128 "Concerning Rebirth", CW 9, i, par. 234

129 "A Study in the Process of Individuation", CW 9, i, par. 562f. _

130 Quoted in William James, p.470

131 Quoted in Martin Buber, *Ekstatische Konfessionen* (Leipzig, 1921), p.52

132 Lothar Schreyer, *Die Mystik der Deutschen* (Hamburg, 1933), p.52

133 Ibid., p.69

134 Joseph Bernhart, ed., *Eine Deutsche Theologie* (Leipzig, 1920), p.103

135 Leopold Naumann, ed., *Johann Tauler Predigten* (Leipzig, 1923), pp.147, 245

136 Nicholas Berdyaev, *Spirit and Reality* (London, 1939), p.145

137 Evelyn Underhill, ed., *The Cloud of Unknowing* (London, 1946), p.13

138 Ibid., p.19

139 Ibid., p.22

140 Ibid., pp.182f.

141 J.M. Cohen, tr., *The Life of Saint Teresa of Avila* (Harmondsworth, 1957), p.119

142 Ibid., p.140

143 E. Allison Peers, ed., *The Complete Works of Saint John of the Cross* (London, 1943), Vol.1, p.10

144 Martin Buber, *Ekstatische Konfessionen*, p.44

145 Martin Buber, *Tales of the Hasidim: Early Masters*, p.253

146 Ibid., pp.275f.

146a D.H. Lawrence, *Essays* (London, 1936)

147 Cf. Kaethe Wolf-Gumpold, *William Blake*, (London, 1969), p.137

148 *Letters*, ed. G. Adler and A. Jaffé, Vol.2 (Princeton and London, 1976), p.467

149 *Letters*, Vol.1 (1973), p.247

150 *Letters*, Vol.2, pp.466f.

151 *Bericht über das Seminar von Prof. Dr. J.W. Hauer* (privately pub., Zürich, 1932), p.146. Now in *Spring* 1976, p.30

152 William James, p.410

153 Radhakrishnan and Moore, p.575

154 CW 12, par. 15

155 Erich Neumann, in his posthumous *The Child*, tr. Ralph Manheim (New York, 1973), makes an interesting contribution to the problem. He says (p.48): "Even after the ego has become independent and consciousness has been systematized and stabilized, they are neither constant nor absolutely necessary to the biopsychic totality. The child lives without them, and so does the sleeper or the man who is 'absent' in psychic disorder or ecstasy. On its return to waking consciousness from such an absence, the ego is able — potentially — to bring back an experience from a state in which it was suspended, that is, seemingly nonexistent."

156 *Letters*, Vol.2, p.561

157 Daisetz T. Suzuki, *Zen and Japanese Culture* (New York, 1959), p.78

158 Radhakrishnan and Moore, pp.46f.

Index

active imagination, 9
Adler, Alfred, 103
agorophobia, 52, 53, 56
Agrippa of Nettesheim, 34
Aeschylus, 154
Albertus Magnus, 126
alchemy (*see also opus magnus; temenos*), 26-7, 30; *aurum non vulgi,* 83; double nature of, 32; *filius macrocosmi,* 24; *filius/a philosophorum,* 24, 48; *krater,* 21, 54, 83, 84; Jung's study of, 9, 85, 138; *lapis,* 9, 24, 25, 27; *nigredo,* number symbolism, 43; *opus contra naturam,* 27, 41, 84; *prima materia,* 27, 30; quicksilver, 28, 168; *scintillae,* 34-5, 49; symbolism, 9, 24; *unus mundus,* 149
amnesia, 121, 152
analysis (*see also* psychoanalysis): inner education in, 68
analyst(s) (*see also* countertransference; transference) choice of, 82; disagreements between, 107-8; relation with patients, 67, 81, 92
analytical-reductive approach, 28, 106-7, 113
anamnesis, 127; of Christ, 143
anima, 5, 8, 81, 97, 135; projectic 53, 97
anima mundi ("World Soul"), 34,
animus, 8, 41-2, 55, 81, 97, 135
Answer to Job, 9, 99, 136
Apollo, 32
Apostle Thomas, Acts of, 132
Aquarius, aeon of, 100-1, 115
Aquinas, Thomas, 126, 168

archetypal images, 5, 13; and critical periods of development, 74; invasion by, 93; Jung's exposure to, 90, 91; of parents, 17; personal experience of, 13
archetypes (*see also* collective unconscious), 5, 16; and archetypal images, 7; as mediators, 12; as regulators or dominants, 6, 12; and memory, 121; of incest, 52; of meaning, 78; of memory, 122; of mother, 6; of self, 140; quasi-consciousness of, 34-5; 'paradoxical quality' of, 110
Arnold, Matthew, 151
art: applications of Jung's ideas in, 12-13; and inner reality, 65; Jung on, 64; perspective in, 98
Artemis, 32
Asklepios, 32
Association of Jungian Analysts (Alternative Training), 117
Association Studies, 116
Augustine, St, 126-7, 159
Aurobindo, Sri, 163
aurum non vulgi, 83

Baal Shem, (the founder of Hasidism), 150
Backster, Cleve, 150, 151
Bardo Thödol (*Tibetan Book of the Dead*), 143-4
Bartlett, F.C., 120
Baruch, of Mezbish, Rabbi, 130
Bergson, Henri, 97, 145
Bhagavad Gita, 144-5, 156
Bindu, 135
Binswanger, Ludwig, 98

birth of self, *see under* self, the

Blake, William, 162

boar, dream of, 55, 56, 57

Böhme, Jacob, 159-60

Bohr, Niels, 108, 109

Bollingen, Jung's tower at, 1

Bose, Sir Jagadis Chandra, 150-1

Brahma, 131, 162

Bruno, Giordano, 126

Buber, Martin, 150, 165

Buddha/Buddhism, 144-5, 156, 157,
    163; Dhyana, 138; Mahayana, 157;
    Zen, 157, 164, 166-7

causal viewpoint, 4

chakras, 71

child/parent relationship, 7

child, symbolical meaning of, 23-4,
    25, 26, 35, 48; final stages of
    coniunctio, 58; Jung on, 49

Chiron, 32, 70

Christian concepts and rituals, 9

Cicero, 124-5

clairvoyance, 10

claustrophobia, 35-7, 39, 45

Cloud of the Unknowing, 160

"coincidentia oppositorum", 41

collective unconscious (*see also*
    archetypes; unconscious), 5-8, 15;
    as "super conciousness", 129-30

complementarity, 108, 112-14

complexes, 2

Confucius, 157

coniunctio, 44, 52-60; anticipation of,
    54; outer and inner aspects, 59, 84;
    primal, 53

consciousness in unconscious, 33-5

consensus omnium, 158

countertransference (*see also*
    transference), 67, 82, 92

cryptomnesia, 121

cultural unrest, 64, 100

cure, 70, 71

Dante, 154, 166, 169

Dee, John, 126

déja vu, 133-6

Demeter, 48

de Montet, Charles, 113

deus absconditus, 90

Dhammapada, 157

Digha-Nikaya, 144

Dionysius the Areopagite, 159

dissociation, 21

Dorn, Gerhard, 77

"dominants", archetypes as, 6, 12

dragon, fight with, 74

dreams: "big", 35; children's 20;
    compensatory function of, 5;
    creative function of, 5; Jung's,
    137-8, 147; mandala symbols in, 8;
    mythological images in, 6; of birth,
    26; of boar, 55, 56, 57; of death, 26;
    of 'ground plan', 75, 76, 77; of
    initiation, 36, 39, 44, 47; of rape,
    54, 56, 57; of fore knowledge, 136;
    of flying saucers, 139; of two houses,
    138; of mirror, 138

drugs, psychedelic, 146-7

Eckhardt, Meister, 159

Edda, 43

ego: integration, 52-61; in the
    unconscious, 33-5; and non-ego,
    15-18, 23, 56, 60; surrender to self,
    158-63

egolessness, 158, 162

ego-personality, exaggerated, 36

Egyptian *Book of the Dead*, 143

Elimelekh of Lizhensk, Rabbi, 161

Eliot, T.A., 148

enantiodromia, 30, 32n

Ennead, Egyptian, 43

Eros, 83, 84, 99-101

ESP (extra-sensory perception), 10

Eucharist, 132

existentialism, 66

extraversion, 3

faeces as symbol, 30

Farid ud-din Attar, 161

father: great, 56, 57; incestuous
    fantasies of, 52; negative, 18, 60
feminine individuality, 58
femininity, unconscious, 38, 41
Ficino, Marsilio, 128-9
filius macrocosmi, 24
filius/a philosophorum, 24, 48
fitness, psychic, 75
Flournoy, Thédore, 121
Fludd, Robert, 126
Flying Saucers, 139-40
Fordham, Michael, 16, 22, 50, 114
forgetting (*see also* remembering),
    151-64 *passim*; in Greek thought,
    152-3; in Indian thought, 155-8; in
    Islamic mysticism, 157-8, 161; in
    Jewish mysticism, 161; in Western
    mysticism, 157-61; in shamanism,
    154-5; Jung's interest in, 152, 158
Freud, Sigmund: and Adler, 103; and
    Jung, 2, 3, 103, 115; his courage,
    89-90; his pioneering insights, 67,
    68; his rational approach, 106-7,
    109, 114; on dreams, 7
Freudian psychology, *see*
    psychoanalysis
functional types, 3

Gaia, 122
Gnosticism, Christian, 9
Goethe, J.W. von, 135
"golden flower", 59
Govinda, Lama Anaganka, 143
"ground plan" in dream, 75, 76, 77

Handel's *Messiah*, 25
Hasidism, 130, 150, 158, 161
Hatha Yoga, 131
Hauer, Wilhelm, 71, 162
Heidegger, Martin, 165-6
Hëisenberg, W., 98, 115
Heraclitus, 32
Herakles, 32
Hesse, Hermann, 101
Hesychasm, 159

"hierophant", 35
hieros gamos, 44
hiranya-gharba, 49
homo quadratus, 107
homo totus (*see also* self; wholeness),
    77
hortus conclusus, 76

I Ching, 10, 93-6, 99, 115; interest of
    young people in, 101
identification, 20, 27
illness (*see also* neurotic symptoms): as
    result of divine interference, 32
incest: archetype of, 52; father's
    fantasies, 52; negative, 53, 54,
    59-60; positive, 53, 54, 55, 56;
    symbolic nature of, 3, 107
individuation (*see also* self, the;
    wholeness), 4, 15, 24, 26, 77; and
    individualism, 8-9; and instinct,
    110; and neurotic symptoms, 70,
    139; preconditions of, 25
"inexactitude", problem of, 11
initiation, 155; dream, 36, 39, 44, 47
instinct and individuation, 110
Integration of the Personality, The,
    33
*Introduction to a Science of
    Mythology* (Jung Kerenyi), 34
introversion, 3, 31
Iyer, V. Subrahamanya, 162

Jaffé, Aniela, 109
James, William, 134, 163
Janet, Pierre, 152
Jewish identity, 119
Jewish mysticism, *see* Hasidism
Jewish patients, 108
John of the Cross, St, 160-1
Jones, Ernest, 90, 115
Jordan, Pascual, 109, 110
Jung, C.G., 88-102 *passim*;
    alchemical studies, 9; on art, 64;
    author's encounters with, 1-2,
    88-93; dreams of, 137-8, 147; and

Jung, *cont.*,
  Freud, 2, 3, 103, 115; honorary
    doctorate of science, 13;
    importance of religion to, 9-10;
    letters, 90, 92, 164; on life after
    death, 145, 147, 148-9;
    misunderstandings of, 10;
    personality, 96; and Pueblo
    Indians, 66; scientific conscience,
    163; style, 11-12; works, *see under
    individual titles*
Jungian approach: depreciation of,
  105; London Group, 103-4;
  original, 104

Kabbala, 130, 131, 132, 143
Kandinski, Vasily, 65, 133
katabasis, 153-4
Kenshin (Zen master), 164
Kerenyi, Carl, 32, 122
Klee, Paul, 65, 133
Kore (*see also* child, symbolic
  meaning of), 48
Koronis, 32
krater, alchemical, 21, 54, 83, 84
Kundalini Yoga, 71

lapis (philosophers' stone), 9, 24, 25,
  27
Layard, John, 55
Leibniz, Gottfried Wilhelm von, 126
Lesmosyne (Lethe), 123, 152-4
libido, 3
life after death, 145-9, 164
Locke, John, 119
"logos", 119
"logos of the unconscious" (*see also*
  unconscious), intellectual activity
  of, 35, 38, 42, 49, 50
Lonergan, Bernard, 102
lumen naturae (Paracelsus), 34, 49
Luria, A.R., 125

Macbeth, 154
Machaon, 32
Magdeburg, Mechthild von, 159

"magic flower" motif in child's
  drawing, 20
Mahabharata, 156
mandala, 8, 20, 21, 76
mantic methods, 10
Marc, Franz, 65, 133
Markandeya, 79
mass: double aspect of, 96; for the
  dead, 143
materialism, 65
Matisse, Henri, 95
Matsyendranath, 131-2
meaning (and loss of meaning),
  62-87 *passim*; archetype of, 78
meditation, objects of, 21
Meier, C.A., 32, 108
Memories, Dreams, Reflections, 3,
  90, 91, 106, 133, 134, 145, 148-9
memory, *see* remembering
Meredith, George, 153
Messiah, Handel's, 25
metapsychological premises, 104,
  106-8, 111-14
Milarepa, 81
"miraculous birth", *see* child,
  symbolical meaning of
Mithras, 43
Mnemosyne, 122, 127, 152-4
mnemotechnics, 123-7
Montet, Charles de, 113
Moore, Henry, 98
mother: archetype of, 7; "bad", 53;
  great, 54; negative, 18, 36, 37
Mysterium Coniunctionis, 78
mysticism: Islamic, 157; Western, 157

Nagarjuna, 157
Narayana, 79, 80
Narenda, 113
nature, the "work" against, 27, 41, 84
Neoplatonism, 159
Neumann, Erich, 31, 47, 50, 52, 170;
  on feminine psychology, 58-9
neurotic symptoms, 39-40, 46, 68-73,
  140-1; constructive aspect, 69;
  numinosity, 72, 73

New Testament, 142-3
night sea journey, 74
nigredo, 30
nothingness, 159-160
Novalis (F.L.F. von Hardenberg), 43, 45
number symbolism, 43-4, 50-1
numinosity, 11, 85, 155; of human relationships, 81; of unconscious, 129; transpersonal, 133

Old Testament, 141, 150
On the Psychology and Pathology of So-Called Occult Phenomena, 2, 33, 120-1
opposites: interplay of, 3, 4; union of (*see also* wholeness), 24, 51
opus contra naturam, 27, 41, 84
opus magnum, 24, 26, 32, 40, 82, 139
Orestes, 154
Orphic mysteries, 127-8, 153
Ouranos, 122
Outline of Psychoanalysis (Freud), 7

paleolithic man, 122
Pali Canon, 144, 157
Paracelsus, 34
parapsychology, 94, 99
parental identification, 20
parental images, 17, 21, 22, 26
parental projections, 20
participation mystique, 66
Passover, 132
Pasternak, Boris, 95
Pauli, Wolfgang, 113
"pearl of great price", 132
perspective in art, 98
personal equation, 108, 112
Philo Judaeus, 158-9
philosphers' stone, *see lapis*
"philosphical" process in unconscious, *see* "logos of the unconscious"
phobias, 71-2; agoraphobia, 52, 53, 56; claustrophobia, 35-7, 39, 45
Piaget, Jean, 16
Picasso, Pablo, 13

Pisces, aeon of, 101
plants, consciousness in, 150-1
Plato, 84, 123; and forgetting, 127-30; and memory, 152-3
Plaut, A.B.J., 32
Plotinus, 159, 166
politics, application of Jung's ideas in, 12, 13
positivist psychology, 129
Prajapati hymn, 49
prehistoric man, 122
prima materia, 27, 30
projection, 9, 12, 60, 92; in alchemy, 9, 27, 85; of anima, 53; and inner/outer correspondence, 97; parental, 20, 22; of self, 79, 84; and transference, 83
Proust, Marcel, 136-7
psyche: constructive powers of, 85; reality of, 93-9; as self-regulating system, 4, 17, 73, 92
psychic energy, 4
psychoanalysis (*see also* Freud), 67-8; and analytical psychology, 104-7, 109-10, 115-16; and forgetting, 120, 152
Psychological Types, 3, 103, 116 (*see above under* "On the ...")
Psychology of Dementia Praecox, The, 2
psychometry, 149, 150
Psychopathology of Everyday Life (Freud), 120
psychotherapy, 62-87 *passim*; and analysis, 104-5; character of, 67
puberty, 74
Pueblo Indians, 66
purification, 28, 29
Pythagoreans, 123; dream theories, 42

quicksilver in alchemy, 26, 168

Radhakrishnan, Sarvelpalli, 156
Rahner, karl, 168

rape dream, 54, 56, 57
Rashi (Bible Commentator), 142
regression, 31
religion: *a priori* meanings in, 75; and
    integration of psyche, 9; Jung's
    interest in, 9-10; personal
    experience of eternal images, 13
religious symbols, 9-10
remembering (*see also* forgetting),
    119-51 *passim*; archetype of
    memory, 122; collective memory,
    119-20; in Jewish throught, 165;
    "memory of the future", 138-9; in
    New Testament, 142-3; in Old
    Testament, 141-3; and personal
    identity, 119; and psychoanalysis,
    120; techniques, 123-7
repression, 120, 137, 152
repudiation, trauma of, 20, 29
resistance, 68
Rigveda, 49
Rilke, Rainer Maria, 135
rite de passage, 154-5
Rosenzweig, Franz, 117
Rumi, Jalal-ud-din, 129

schizophrenia, 2
scintillae, 34
self, the, 15; archetype of, 140; dream
    of face of, 77, 78, 138-9; and
    empirical personality, 76;
    emergence in childhood, 16-23,
    30-1; flying saucers as image of,
    140; as image of wholeness, 17, 21,
    22; involved in own birth, 31, 48-9;
    in Plato, 129-30; surrender of ego
    to, 158-63; as transcendental
    subject of cognition, 49; in
    Upanishads, 131
self regulation: in life of nations and
    epochs, 64; in psyche, 4, 17, 73, 92
sexuality and dream interpretation, 28
shadow, 12
Shakespeare, William, 154
Shakti, 44

shamanism, 154-5
Shelomo of Karlin, Rabbi, 161
Shereshevskii (memory prodigy),
    125-6, 152
Shiva, 44
Simonides of Ceos, 124-5
Society of Analytical Psychology
    (London), 103
"Song of the Pearl", 132
spooks, 149
Stein, Frau von, 135
Studies in Word Association, 2, 121
suffering, Jung on, 90
Sufism, 161
sulcus primigenius, 21
"sun's phallus", 6
sunyata, 143, 157, 162
"*souvenir pur*", 145
suprapersonal totality (*see also* self;
    wholeness), 76, 77
symbols: dynamic effect of, 5; Freud's
    view of, 4, 107; Jung's view of, 4,
    11, 111; as transformers of energy, 5
Symbols of Transformation, 3, 137
symptoms, neurotic, *see* neurotic
    symptoms
synaesthesia, 125
synchronicity, 10, 80, 93-4, 108, 116,
    151
synthetic-constructive approach, 28,
    106-7, 113
systole and diastole, 120

Tantric philosophy, 44, 71
Tao, 157
Tauler, Johannes, 159
Tavistock Lectures, 121
techniques, analytic, 104, 106, 111, 114
Teilhard de Chardin, P., 149
teleological viewpoint, 4
telepathy, 115
temenos (*see also* mandala), 20, 21,
    22, 35, 36; analyst as, 83; maternal
    52, 53, 54, 55, 69; square, 59;
    symbolised by house or garden, 76

Tennyson, Alfred Lord, 133
Teresa of Avila, St, 160
Themistocles, 152
Thomas à Kempis, 159
Tibetan Book of the Dead (*Bardo Thödol*), 143-4
Tibetan Book of the Great Liberation, 132
Tillich, Paul, 167
totality, *see* wholeness
transcendental consciousness, centre of, 33
transference (*see also* counter-transference), 20, 45, 53, 54, 67, 82; "internalized", 60
Trinity: image in man, 127; Jung on, 9
Trophonios, 153-4
typology, Jung's, 3, 92

"uncertainty relationship", 112
unconscious: collective, *see* collective unconscious; constructive/creative function of, 4, 36, 40, 92; intellectual activity of, 2, 33-5; "logos" of, 35, 38, 49, 50; as multiple consciousness, 34; obsolete use of term, 129; prospective nature of, 2, 4, 50; timeless quality of, 166
Undiscovered Self, The, 12
Ungrund, 159-60
Unio mystica, 159
Unus Mundus, 149, 151
Upanishads, 74, 131, 156, 164
urine as symbol, 30
urobouros, 59,60
uterus symbol, 41

vas bene clausum, 21
Vedas/Vedanta, 144, 156, 163; Rigveda, 49
Virgil, 153

weihaug, sutra of, 138
Whitman, Walt, 136
wholeness (totality) (*see also* self, the; individuation): in child, 17, 21-2; child as symbol of, 24; development in child, 26; dynamics of controversion, 73; symbolic expression of, 8
"wilderness", perception of world as, 36, 45
Wilhelm, Richard, 95, 102
Williams, Charles, 146
"wise old man", 42, 45
"wise old woman", 36
Wolff, Toni, 103
"Women's lib", 100
Wordsworth, William, 132-3
"World Soul" (*anima mundi*), 34, 49
Worringer, Wilhelm, 64
wounded healer, 32, 40, 140

yantras, 20
Yeats, W.B., 165

Zen Buddhism, 157, 164, 166£7
Zeus, 32, 122
Zurich School of Analytical Psychology, 103-4